The Language of the Badger

Badger

A year of personal encounters with the wildlife on our doorstep

The fifth book in the 'Simple Life' series

by Mary-Jane Houlton

Other books by Mary-Jane Houlton

The 'Simple Life' series
Just Passing Through (Book 1)
A Simple Life (Book 2)
The Turning of the Seasons (Book 3)
The Constant Traveller (Book 4)

How to be a House-Sitter

Contents

Author's note

Books are so much more than pen and paper. For those of us who love them they are companions, precious friends offering a safe haven when the world is too worrying or too frantic and we need a place where we can escape.

The Language of the Badger was never meant to become a book. I began this project purely for myself. The long winter months have always been a trial for me and I needed something to lighten them, to keep me positive and engaged. I set aside one morning each week, usually a Sunday, and spent a few hours by the fire, learning more about something that had intrigued me during the week. Surprisingly quickly this Sunday morning ritual became important to me, something to look forward to, a time just for me. Its beneficial effects spread out into the week, giving me a new focus, opening my eyes to the small wonders that surrounded me. I realised how often I looked without really seeing and how much I was missing out on.

Winter turned to spring and my spirits lifted of their own accord. It occurred to me that I no longer needed my questions to cheer me up but still I kept scribbling away each Sunday. I had become attached to the way it made me feel: excited and curious, better connected to the natural world around me and more thoughtful about my place in the wider scheme of things.

As my notepad grew full a small voice in my head suggested that this book should be shared, not hidden away in a drawer by my bed. And so my random scribblings were knocked into shape and finally I had my book, one which holds a special place in my heart. I don't pretend to be an expert on any of the subjects covered, simply someone who wanted to know more about her world, and any mistakes or errors are all my own. I am so pleased to share what I have learnt with you and hope that it might become a companion book for you in the same way that it has for me.

INTRODUCTION

As a child I was naturally curious. Everything was new to me and there was so much to discover. I don't think I was unusual; it was just the natural curiosity of a child. I was so hungry for knowledge and understanding that I drove my parents to distraction, always asking why, where or how. I couldn't help myself; the questions popped out of my mouth seemingly of their own volition.

All these years later that natural curiosity about the world around me seems muted and that bright-eyed child a distant memory. I find this strange as we live in a digital age where all knowledge is literally at our fingertips. I have the means to answer any query I can dream up, and yet the desire to ask questions seems to have dwindled. Instead I feel smothered by an overload of information that is not of my choosing, is more often than not deeply depressing, and which leaves me weary. My brain has so many things that it needs to process that it no longer has the capacity for whimsical questions or the energy to pursue the answers.

Curiosity is a wonderful thing though, something that we all need in our lives. The dictionary describes it as an eager wish to know or to learn about something and whilst some definitions can be stilted, those words struck a chord with me. I wanted to wake up in the morning feeling excited about what my day might bring. I felt a pang of longing for that sense of childish wonder that I had been too young to appreciate fully. For my own well-being I needed to feel more positive about the world I lived in and find some way to restore a sense of balance.

It seemed to me that reconnecting with my natural sense of curiosity would be the first small step along that road. It was time to open my eyes and my mind and let the small things in life beguile me once more. I set myself the challenge of learning something new each week, asking one simple question and letting the answer take me where it would. If no question came to mind it would be enough just to notice something new and to appreciate it for its own sake. I didn't expect this resolution to be a life-changing experience or an overly time-consuming habit, I was just hoping for a small part of each week in my everyday life that would become special.

I have always turned to the natural world for succour, and it soon became clear that my questions reflected this natural affinity for the landscape and the animals that were around me. I learned why butterflies danced and where the wind came from, how we can read the stars and all about the secret life of trees. One question often led to another, and an innocent, childish thought sometimes took me off at a tangent that only an adult would consider.

After just a few months of indulging my curiosity I found that it was not possible to be half-hearted about the process. The more I learnt, the more I wanted to learn. I soon came to the conclusion that curiosity didn't kill the cat, it made its life far more interesting.

From my own experience I am now a firm believer of the many benefits that arise from indulging our natural curiosity, but the science backs up my personal feelings. We retain more information when we actively choose to learn rather than being fed an endless stream of largely unnecessary data that goes in one ear and out of the other. Curiosity activates the same area of the brain as when we accomplish something, stimulating the release of dopamine, the 'feel-good' hormone, and as a result offers a level of protection against anxiety and depression. A curious mind is the psychological equivalent of a healthy heartbeat, a nurturing link between the mind and the body.

This book is a chronological record of my questions and the resulting answers, beginning in January and running on month by month to December. It is set against the backdrop of our cabin home near the Pyrenees for the winter months and on our boat in the Netherlands for the summer months but it is not a travelogue, the focus being more on the animals that we meet on the way rather than our personal journey. There were some weeks when I couldn't find a question, but was content to simply become more aware of something beautiful or strange. Some questions provoked a longer answer than others, whilst for some the answer remained elusive. It also provides a record of a year where, much to my surprise, my life has been quietly changed. Curiosity, my old childhood friend, that voice in my head who had such a zest for life, is now my constant companion. All too often I have embarked upon a new resolution for a new year and it has fallen by the wayside. Not this time. My sense of curiosity has become strong; it thrives and is a part of me once more. When my year comes to an end I know I shall keep on asking questions and being delighted by the answers.

JANUARY

A harsh and stark beauty awaits those who brave

the winter chill

Purr-fect

'You aren't being very helpful.'

My remark was addressed to Spot, our cat. I was outside, the wooden bench by our front door doubling up as my office as a weak winter sun had made an unexpected appearance and I couldn't bear to be inside. I still needed a thick fleece but the sky was blue and I could almost fool myself into thinking that spring was around the corner, despite the fact that we were barely into the new year. My notepad and various bits of paper were spread out in front of me and the cat had appeared within seconds of me sitting down, outlining a faint trail of damp paw prints over my scribbles and headbutting my hand as I tried to write. When that didn't elicit the required amount of attention she stretched herself out across the table, belly up, rolling around in supreme confidence that I would find her irresistible, purring loudly.

My husband Michael and I lead quite a nomadic life but if anywhere is home, this is it. Let me introduce you to Le Shack, a one-room, off-grid wooden cabin in the south west of France that was a shell when we bought it in 2020. It had no kitchen, no bathroom, no bedroom, consisting literally of just four walls. The loo was, and still is, a bucket in the shed. There is no electricity; all power is generated from solar panels with a generator as a back-up but we are connected to mains water. The cabin is situated in one corner of a large field, part of the five acres of land that came with the property. This wonderful wilderness in the middle of nowhere is reflected in so many of the questions and answers in this book.

When we bought the cabin, we also inherited Spot, a black and white half-wild moggy with a big white spot on her left flank. I suspect her previous French owner would have given her a rather more imaginative name, but we never knew what it was and so Spot she became. Much as we love animals, having had many of our own over the years, we didn't want a cat. We spent at least half the year travelling and couldn't commit to looking after her. It soon became obvious, thankfully, that Spot didn't need looking after and didn't regard herself as 'our' cat. This was her home before it became ours, and she regarded humans as transient, merely passing through. She was a prodigious mouser and, if ever the mice became scarce when we were away, she had an alternative home further down the valley with another set of humans who could be relied upon to put out some food if she made enough of a fuss.

Despite being a very independent cat there was no doubt that she was glad of our company and each autumn when we returned she was ecstatic, following us around, jumping on our laps the minute we sat down anywhere, including the outside loo unless you could deflect her in time. At times I could even hear her through the door when I was in bed and I knew she would be sat on the mat outside, nose almost touching the door itself, purring away for all she was worth.

Why do cats purr? I thought I knew the answer to this question but I soon realised that the answer was not as simple as I had thought.

Whilst cats certainly do purr as a sign of pleasure, it would be more accurate to say that they use it as a form of communication in a much wider sense. They are born blind and deaf and begin purring a few days after birth, to let their mothers know where they are and to attract attention at feeding time. Purring continues into adulthood but it isn't a given that all cats will purr and some are more vocal than others. They will purr when they are injured, or after a stressful event, and vets have noticed that cats will even purr as they are dying and being put to sleep.

Purring in these types of situations has a completely different function. Research has suggested that purring is a soothing mechanism, in much the same way as a child might suck his or her thumb. It goes even further and suggests that the vibrations caused in producing the sound can self-heal, helping to mend broken bones, repair wounds and torn tendons, easing pain and swelling, and it could explain why cats can survive high falls and have fewer complications after surgery than dogs. It sounds far-fetched to suggest that a healthy purr contributes to a cat's nine lives but it is well known that frequencies play a part in therapeutic healing for humans. Bone responds to 25–50Hz and soft tissues to 100Hz. Given that cat purring ranges from a frequency of 20–150Hz, it doesn't seem unreasonable to conclude that it could have a beneficial effect.

There is an old English proverb about cats and their nine lives: *'For three he plays, for three he strays and for the last three he stays.'* It encapsulates something of the character of felines, their playfulness and their independent nature, but it doesn't really explain why they are able to survive some of the dangerous situations that their inherently curious nature lands them in.

I have often watched Spot as she has jumped down from the large ash tree that stands over our cabin, landing with effortless grace on the roof. Cats are hunters and they have strong, muscular legs designed to allow them to jump and climb. A cat's skeletal system is made up of 30 vertebrae, and they lack a collarbone which further adds to their flexibility. Even when they do misjudge a leap and fall they can absorb considerable impact which in turn minimises the damage. There are numerous accounts of cats jumping from buildings and surviving against the odds, one well-known example being a cat in New York City who fell from a window on the 32nd floor. It ended up with a chipped tooth and a collapsed lung but after only two days in an animal hospital it was safely returned home to convalesce.

I suspect there is no aspect of life on our planet that hasn't intrigued a scientist over the centuries and the question of how cats can survive the type of fall that would kill or seriously disable another animal, or indeed a human, has not escaped their scrutiny. In 1894 a French physiologist named Étienne-Jules Marey used a chronophotographic camera, which captures images of a moving subject at regular time intervals and superimposes them on the same image, to capture what happened when he held his cat upside down and dropped it. It's hard not to imagine a man in a white coat repeatedly dropping his long-suffering cat from his balcony just so he could study the fall in minute detail when you read about an experiment like this. Not an image to dwell on.

Thanks to a highly developed vestibular system in their inner ear, which controls balance and orientation, cats have the ability to recognise which way is up and then twist themselves into a position so that they can land on all fours. Research published in the *Journal of the American Veterinary Medical Association* in 1987 analysed the records of 132 cats who had fallen from buildings. They found that the distance of the fall will also affect the severity of the injuries, although not in the way you might expect. After the equivalent of seven storeys, the number of injuries actually decreases. It gives the cat time to relax, allowing them to use their body almost as a parachute. Yet again another image comes to mind, a cartoon character of a cat flying through the air, legs akimbo, eyes popping out of its head and its fur standing on end.

By now Spot had crawled onto my lap, still purring. I closed my eyes and enjoyed the sensation of her warm body against mine.

'What a little miracle you are,' I said quietly, and she blinked at me in silent agreement.

As we sat there contentedly in the morning sunshine I didn't need to turn to science to know that I found her company pleasing and that the rumble of her purring had a relaxing effect on me. I later found a charming interpretation in the strangest of places, the website for Whiskas cat food, which has all sorts of interesting cat information on it. Rather whimsically, it suggested that purring was a feline lullaby, one that soothed the soul of both the singer and the listener.

So now when my little cat jumps on my lap and purrs while I stroke her silky fur I like to think that we are both benefiting, a mutually soothing and calming interlude. Satisfaction guaranteed to both parties. And it also goes to prove that it is worth asking a question even if you think you know the answer.

The naming of things

Imagine a winter's evening as the sun sinks below the horizon and the bright-white snow on the distant Pyrenees fades into the shadows. The sky is the colour of a blood-red orange and thousands of starlings are swooping and diving, rising and falling, blocks of shadow and light constantly changing, each image lasting no more than a second.

It is thought that these distinctive flight patterns, a prelude to roosting for the night, are a form of protection against predators. There is safety to be had in large numbers and the constant movement makes it harder for birds of prey to pick off individual starlings. However, whilst they may not be calling or singing, the beat of thousands of wings in unison generates its own sound, a background hum or murmur, and this is why this natural phenomenon is called a murmuration.

Ten minutes later and it was all over. The birds had disappeared, safely hidden away in the trees until dawn, and the skies seemed empty without them. Intrigued by the idea of how we refer to collections of birds, I decided to research it further and soon realised that I had opened a bird's version of Pandora's box. It seemed that no species had been left out and that people had been creating names and compiling lists of collective nouns for centuries.

One of the oldest of these lists was published anonymously in 1486, and had the rather splendid title of *The Compaynys of Beestys and Fowlys.* Everyone assumed it had been written by a man, but there is some evidence to suggest that it was written by a woman called Juliana Barnes. In those days women were not afforded the same freedoms as men, but she loved to study and to write and, having retreated to a nunnery, found an environment where she could indulge her passion.

Some of these collective nouns for birds have changed over the years, and others have been added, so the list is now a very long one and there is often more than one noun to choose from for each bird. The list below is my top 20 and provides an insight into the whimsical world of the naming of things.

A confusion of chiff chaffs
A trembling of finches
A parcel of linnets
A chime of wrens
A mischief of magpies
A scold of jays
A deceit of lapwings
An invisibleness of ptarmigans
A pitying of turtle doves
A booby of nuthatches

A wisp of snipes
A quilt of elders
A worm of robins
A wake of buzzards
A fling of sandpipers
A congress of eagles
A charm of hummingbirds
A clattering of jackdaws
A parliament of owls
A prattle of parrots

Where do these names come from? Many are descriptive of a particular physical attribute, the way a bird flies or sings, and also from the way they behave, a perfect example being a commotion of coots. Others are born from a more emotional response, for example a flamboyance of flamingos. As always folklore and traditional beliefs have their part to play, a contribution that is not always accurate or fair. Groups of crows have been described as a mob, horde or, rather unfairly, a murder, the latter commonly used since medieval times when peasants feared that the birds were emissaries of death sent by the devil or were even witches in disguise.

These collective nouns are charming and quirky but they have no scientific structure or base. Do they serve any real purpose other than to charm and amuse us?

I thought about this for a while and came to the conclusion that the naming of things does matter. Our connection to the natural world is strengthened if we can put a name to a particular bird or animal, not just as a species but also collectively. If we are aware of their habits and behaviour a link is established and they matter more to us. I thought of skylarks singing as I walked over the hills of Wales for so many years, a glorious uplifting anthem in the skies, and knew that I wouldn't forget that they were described collectively as an 'exaltation'. In contrast, a scientific name, presumably in Latin, would all too easily be forgotten.

As these names become part of my vocabulary, so the birds that they refer to become part of my world, something to care about, to nurture and protect. It's no different to the way in which we react to our own fellow humans. It's easy to dismiss a stranger, someone that we know nothing about, but once we put a name to a face or a family there is a connection, which can lead to a relationship and from there we start to look out for each other. Names matter.

The sound of silence

On a recent trip back to the UK we took a city break in Bath. We enjoyed our stay, and it is indeed a beautiful city, but after a few days I found myself desperate for respite from the seemingly endless stream of people and cars in and around the city and the noise that always comes with them, a never-ending barrage of energy and sound. Each time we return to France and the peace and quiet of our cabin I take a deep breath of silence, as vital as the air in my lungs, let it settle over me like a comfort blanket and feel myself become calm. But is there really such a thing as silence?

In my mind our home is a quiet place, a silent place, and yet I am fooling myself. The natural world is rarely quiet and all I have done is exchange one set of noises for another.

I sat down in the middle of the field the other day with a notepad and pen and wrote a list of everything that I heard over a period of ten minutes: a blackbird chattering, the wind rustling through the bare branches and dislodging a dried leaf that crackled as it fell, a background whine of a chainsaw, the flapping of wings as a crow lifted off from the top of the oak tree nearest the cabin, a dog barking down in the valley, a woodpecker drilling into the bark of a tree, the wing beats of a flock of pigeons above me, the chatter of small birds. At some point the chainsaw stopped and the balance changed, allowing the quieter noises to become clearer. I closed my eyes, let my hearing become my primary sense and heard a rustling in the undergrowth.

My ten minutes came to an end but at no point had there been a time of complete silence. I decided to extend my experiment by another five minutes but it made no difference. Then I decided to try again at different times of day and at night. Even in the darkness, in such isolation, a new set of characters made it their business to keep the silence at bay, owls hooting, a fox or deer barking and more unidentifiable rustling in the woods. Granted there were short interludes of silence, which was at least something, but they never lasted long.

None of these natural noises affected me in the same way

as the noises that are generated by the human race. Nature is rarely silent, always singing or buzzing, scratching or scurrying, but I found it soothing, comforting. Prolonged silence is an absence of all noise, a nothingness, a terrifying void where no life exists and, looking at my collection of lists from my ten-minute listening sessions, a habit which has become addictive, I realised I had never actually wanted silence. All I wanted was a sense of peace and that, thankfully, is easier to find.

Beauty is only skin deep

When did human beings first become obsessed with the notion of beauty? This preoccupation with excellence spills over into so much of the way that we view the world, aspiring always to be the best at everything we do, and to be respected and lauded for it accordingly. We apply these measures of worth not just within our own species, but also to the animals that surround us. We venerate the majesty of the lion and the speed of the cheetah. We are in awe of the sheer size of the elephant, beguiled by the beauty of the hummingbird and kingfisher. Anything that looks soft and cuddly brings a smile to our faces.

But what about the rest of them? What about the creatures who have none of these appealing attributes, who might be regarded as plain and slow, or ugly and weak? Should we ignore them simply because they are ordinary and don't stand out in a crowd? I like to think that most creatures on this planet have something special about them, even though you may have to look hard to find it.

A belly-foot was crawling its way up the outside of one of my terracotta pots, a perfect example of an animal that would never be allowed in the private members' bar for the gifted and the beautiful. This particular mollusc is better known as a snail, and it moves by flattening its body at the belly to form a crawling surface similar to a foot. Its scientific Latin name is *gastropod,* with the first half of the word meaning stomach, or belly, and the latter half meaning foot.

Snails evoke strong emotions in people, often negative, and I allowed myself a moment of uncharitable satisfaction in knowing that its journey would be fruitless as the pot was empty and there would be no feasting on my plants today. To gardeners they are public enemy number one, and generally they are viewed with distaste, no more than a lump of slimy pulp in a shell.

But then I looked more closely at the shell and I noticed two things. Firstly, I could see that it was actually beautiful, the pattern becoming more delicate and intricate the longer I looked at it. The spirals ran in a clockwise direction and this is because most molluscs have a physical bias to the right, in the same way as most humans are right-handed. It is very rare to see the pattern going in the other direction.

The second thought to cross my mind was more practical in nature, an appreciation of how sensible it is to carry one's home upon one's back. It's always there when you need protection, a safe place in which to retreat. We spend much of our lives doing the same thing in a way. We live on a boat for the summer, and our boat goes where we do. In the past we have travelled for long periods of time in camper vans, another home on the move.

Snails are born with their shells, will stay permanently attached to that same structure all their lives, and are unable to live without it. In those first days the shell is soft and fragile, taking time to harden. The young snail eats the egg from which it has just emerged, a meal rich in calcium, and this marks the beginning of a lifetime of searching out calcium-rich foods, vegetables like spinach and broccoli being firm favourites for that reason, so that they can build and maintain their shell. They manufacture the shell themselves from a part of their body called the mantle, each successive layer added to the edge and slowly hardening after it has been formed. In much the same way that a tree can be aged by the number of rings in the trunk, so does the shell record the life history of the snail within.

I began to look at this diminutive garden pest with different eyes. I couldn't help but admire how it was so perfectly adapted to its environment and way of living. Although I am always going to be frustrated when I lose vegetables or plants to a night of nocturnal munching, the snail is just doing what it does naturally, seeking out calcium-rich foods to grow and harden its shell house.

A sparrow flew into a nearby hedge, shifting my attention away from the snail. Now this surely was a perfect candidate for a plain and unexciting creature, very common and with nothing special about it at all. But yet again, once I looked below the surface, there was more to what we call an LBJ (little brown job) than meets the eye. The sparrow can claim the accolade of being the most widely distributed bird on the planet, found in every continent except Antarctica. It is highly adaptable, can flourish in changing environments and has seen the wisdom in using the human species and the world they have built as a way to help it survive. It chooses its own boundaries, largely ignoring ours, as it will live and breed in factories and supermarkets, industrial warehouses and even zoos. It is an opportunistic feeder, fearlessly hoovering up crumbs from tables in restaurants, and has been seen nesting on the 80th floor of the Empire State Building. It's a cheeky opportunist, a survivor, a far more useful character trait than being simply beautiful.

It was becoming clear that there was no such thing as ordinary, but I had one last creature who might prove to be the exception and this was the worm. The worm is essentially a digestive tube with a mouth at one end and an opening for waste matter at the other. They eat decaying plant matter, dragging it down into their burrows where they use their muscly mouths to gum dinner into submission as they have no teeth. Once digested, it is excreted through the other end of the tube as worm casts, little mounds of soil that have been enriched with nutrients and minerals as they pass through the worm. Worms are featureless, no eyes, no ears, and pretty much everyone else in the animal world wants to eat them which isn't exactly something to aspire to. On the plus side, they do have five hearts, which is four more than I do, so you could argue that is quite an achievement for such a simple creature. Also to their credit they have been around for at least 500 million years, which proves they are a survivor, and are quite likely to outlive the human race.

In fact, the humble worm is one of the least dull, least ordinary of all living creatures. Charles Darwin studied them for 38 years and believed that the nutrients that they produce as a by-product of their digestive system play a vital role in the history of the world, a building block on which all life on the planet relies. Scientists can't say exactly how many worms inhabit the Earth but they guess that they number more than the stars in the universe, equating to literally trillions of worms wriggling away beneath the surface, providing us with a fertile soil and an ecosystem that allows us all to flourish.

There is something deeply satisfying about finding the extra-ordinary in the ordinary. I had been asking my questions for only one month and at this stage had no idea of how often I would have moments like this over the coming year, moments when my perspective would be changed and a new understanding and appreciation gained.

FEBRUARY

The wind howls, the rain falls and winter fights to the last breath

Don't wish your life away

It's the first week of February and winter feels as if it will never end. This is my least favourite month of the year but in theory today should be a good day. February 2nd is Candlemas Day and traditionally marks the mid-point between the shortest day and the spring equinox. We can actually see the days getting longer and I know this should be a positive sign but the weather loves to toy with us, the sun peeking through for a day and then rain falling for the next week and dashing our hopes, the fall harder to bear because we had that brief respite.

I know it's wrong to wish my life away but each year I wonder what I can do to brighten these long winter months and speed them on their way. Perhaps history can provide some inspiration. The pagans celebrated the festival of Lupercalia in February, which seems to have been a raucous affair. Young men sacrificed goats on an altar and then ran through the town, naked or sporting animal skins, striking women's palms with goatskin whips. Apparently this would boost fertility or make childbirth easier and so the women were as keen to participate as the men. I like to think it cheered everybody up and gave them something to focus on, but it was banned in 949 by Pope Gelasius who felt it led to sinful behaviour, which I imagine it probably did. He replaced it with Candlemas, the festival of light, honouring the end of winter and the return of longer, lighter days. It is a time when Christians take candles to church and ask for a blessing. With no goats or whips in sight, and everybody keeping their clothes on, it was certainly a far more proper and sober affair, if rather dull in comparison.

The pious pope is also credited with the birth of the pancake tradition as he reputedly gave wafers or flatbreads to pilgrims arriving in Rome. Ever reliable, the pagan tradition offers a far more interesting explanation. They believed that a pancake represented the shape of the sun, a symbol of fertility and prosperity. One custom held that if a farmer wanted a good harvest later in the year he must flip a pancake with his left hand, whilst holding a gold coin in his right hand. I'm guessing that this procured a good harvest. Then he should wrap the coin in the pancake, place it on top of a wardrobe for a year, and give it to the first poor person he comes across once the year is up. I imagine a starving peasant would be grateful for the coin, if not a little confused about the mouldy pancake that came with it.

I resign myself to the fact that goat sacrifices, lighting candles in church and eating pancakes are not going to make the winter seem shorter. However I haven't given up on finding ways to make it less tedious. Andy Beer has written a book called *Every Day Nature*, which in itself is a tonic for the winter months, but he shares his personal solution to making the winter easier to bear. He splits it up into two six-week periods, give or take a day or two, using the winter solstice in December and the spring equinox in March as his start and end dates. Dividing a solid block of time into shorter, manageable sections makes it seem less overwhelming. February 2nd is an important day as it acts as a goal or a milestone; the half-way point has been reached. It seems such a simple thing to do but it works for him and I have found it does the same for me.

We may have organised time into days, weeks and months but it doesn't always accept our rules. Time can drag in winter, an hour feeling longer than it is, the hands of the clock seemingly frozen in place, or at least on a go-slow. My own solution to giving time a bit of a nudge is to find something to take me outside of myself, and I often have to physically go outside to do that. At this time of year, it is the Candlemas Bells, probably better known as snowdrops, that provide the motivation to get some fresh air.

In France these 'bells' are known as *les perce-neiges* because they pierce the snow. The Swiss call them *amselblumli*, the blackbird flower, because they bloom as the blackbirds start to sing. It seems such a delicate flower but is surprisingly tough, designed to withstand cold weather. The tips of the leaves are hardened to enable them to push through snow or hard ground, and their sap contains a form of antifreeze. They might wilt after a frosty night, but they soon bounce back as the temperature rises.

These feisty little plants don't let winter get them down, quite the reverse, and I decide that if they can maintain a positive attitude, so can I. In a few weeks' time they will be ready for splitting into clumps so they can be divided and spread around the garden and that will be an activity to look forward to in March. For now, it's enough to look at the snowdrops and believe that winter is on the run.

There are a number of sayings associated with Candlemas and the turning of the seasons and this is one: 'If Candlemas Day be fair and bright, winter will have another fight. If Candlemas Day brings cloud and rain, winter won't come again.' I'm not a great believer in sayings about the weather; it's just too unpredictable. However, looking out of the window and seeing the grey skies, laden with rain, maybe I'll put my cynicism to one side and hope that today there might just be some credence to the old proverb.

The wild wind

Wild weather always sounds worse at night. In the darkness we are robbed of our sight, and rely on our hearing to tell us what's happening. Tonight the wind was in a foul temper, thrashing around in the trees that surround our cabin. Occasionally there would be a lull, a blessed silence, but then it would begin again, the volume steadily growing until it filled my head, a voice of anger and destruction.

I flinched as a particularly strong gust of wind howled its way across the side of our hill, followed by a hefty thud as yet another wayward branch landed on the roof. Our cabin is sited under a large ash tree, great for shade in summer but not so good in strong winds.

'More cracked tiles to sort out,' I muttered crossly to myself, pulling the pillow over my head in the forlorn hope of making the storm go away. The wind had no intention of leaving just yet and eventually I gave up on any notion of sleeping. Instead I pondered where the wind came from, and how all this energy was created.

Wind is the movement of air, caused by an uneven heating of the Earth by the sun and by the Earth's own rotation. At the Equator the sun warms the water and the land more than elsewhere. This warm air rises, leaving a vacuum, and cooler air is pulled in to fill it. This is the simplest way to describe the wind, a continual balancing of the atmosphere, but when you delve deeper into the science it becomes more complicated.

There is a language that specifically describes wind and how it behaves: high and low pressure systems, prevailing winds and convergence zones, easterlies and westerlies, horse latitudes and the Coriolis effect, the doldrums, the Roaring 40s and the Screaming 60s. This section is not one that is going to baffle either the writer or the reader with too much science, but it soon became obvious that there is far more to the wind than the ability to bring branches down on my roof on a windy night. It is a vital part of the Earth's systems, much as blood and oxygen are part of our own bodies. It can't be seen, has no obvious substance and yet it has enormous power. It carries sailing ships across oceans, can lift buildings and cars in a hurricane and reduce visibility to zero in a sandstorm but, more than this, it permeates every part of our lives: from exploration and leisure, to providing energy and affecting our climate, as well as playing a major role in how and where we grow our food. In all these aspects it has the power to nurture or destroy and, whilst we like to tell ourselves that we have tamed the natural world, we are powerless against whatever the wind chooses to throw at us.

In his book *Where the Wild Winds Are,* Nick Hunt has written a fascinating account of his journey to follow four of Europe's major winds across the continent. In the Alpine valleys of Switzerland he finally catches up with a wind called the 'Foehn', which he describes as a 'continuous roar, a ceaseless bellow of white noise, thundering from the narrow cleft between the slopes ahead'. The Foehn is a wind that gets inside people's heads and affects their mental state and on his journey he hears how it causes irritability, anxiety, depression, lethargy and fatigue. He admits that, despite having heard endless tales of how certain winds can affect the human psyche, he never expected it to happen to him and so it is a shock when he finds himself feeling utterly wretched just at the moment when he expected to feel exhilaration. He had walked miles to find this wind, and now that it had found him, all he wanted was for it to stop.

The wind doesn't just move air around the planet, it also carries whatever might be in that air, whether it be heat, moisture, pollutants, pollen, dust or sand and even volcanic ash. It is in this regard that it can affect our climate and our ability to grow food, even our ability to survive. In 1883 strong winds carried volcanic ash from the eruption of Krakatoa in Indonesia right across the world, causing cold damp summers in Europe for years. In 1986 radioactive materials from the Chernobyl nuclear explosion in Ukraine had a devastating effect within the country itself but particles were carried by the wind to many parts of Europe.

During the 1930s the Great Plains in the US suffered from what was known as the Dust Bowl era. A doomed partnership of intensive farming and a prolonged drought turned the soil to dust. Dust storms were common in the area but on April 14th 1935, a day that came to be known as Black Sunday, one particular storm turned the world dark in the middle of the day, engulfing crops and homes in roiling clouds of dust.

According to the Red Cross, 17 people died from dust pneumonia, where dust clogs up the lungs, and three from suffocation, surely an awful way to die. During the Dust Bowl years half a million people were displaced, many of them farming families who lost their homes and their livelihoods. By 1940, two and a half million people had fled from the Great Plains, unable to survive the consequences of the combination of drought and wind. Personal accounts provide a harrowing insight into how difficult it was to live in such conditions.

'People caught in their own yards grope for the doorstep. Cars come to a standstill, for no light in the world can penetrate that swirling murk... The nightmare is deepest during the storms. But on the occasional bright day and usual gray day we cannot shake from it. We live with the dust, eat it, sleep with it, watch it strip us of possessions...'

Avis D. Carlson, 'Dust', The New Republic, 1 May 1935

Eventually the rains would return and farming practices would learn from their mistakes but many of those people who had the misfortune to live in that area over those dark and windy years would not see the benefit of it.

We have developed the habit of giving the wind a name, according it a place in folklore and myths, elevating it to celebrity status and even a tourist attraction.

The 'Barber' wind that blows across Canada and the US is so cold that it freezes the moisture on anything it touches, including hair and beards. The rather whimsically named 'Pembrokeshire Dangler' comes to visit when winds from Wales and Ireland converge over the Irish Sea, forming a line of continuous showers that 'dangle' over the land from West Wales to Cornwall and Devon. The 'November Witch' describes the severe storms that are a feature of the Great Lakes in North America during November, with winds above 80 mph and 20ft seas. All five of the Great Lakes are a graveyard of boats, with more than 6,000 vessels lost beneath the waves between 1878 and 1897 alone. Equally appalling, it is estimated that 25,000 seafarers have been lost over the last 300 years, most of them falling victim to the November Witch.

I realise how incredibly puny and insignificant I am as a human when I learn that the wind is not constrained by the boundaries of our own planet, or even our own solar system, and that the winds that create such havoc in our world are of little consequence when compared to how the wind blows when it truly flies free.

The strongest winds in our solar system are found on Neptune, where they may reach speeds of 2,100km per hour, but even these pale into insignificance when we step deeper into space. Wind speeds of 14,400km per hour have been recorded on the extrasolar planet of 51 Pegasus.

Back on Earth, our own personal wind, one that would have to content itself with remaining nameless, had finally exhausted itself, and the deep and comforting silence of the night had flowed into the gap that it left behind. After tonight I would regard the wind with fresh eyes, glad to understand it better, but for now, all I wanted to do was savour the peace and drift off to sleep.

Singing my heart out

I first began singing outdoors because I had unwittingly walked into the middle of a group of French hunters and wanted to draw their attention to the fact that I was not a wild boar or deer. Walking into such a situation might sound like a stupid thing to do, but the French hunt, or *la chasse*, is hard to avoid at times. Often we hear gunshot or the hounds barking, or see a procession of off-road jeeps hurtling down the lanes and this gives us an idea of where to avoid. Other times the only clue is when you suddenly find yourself face to face with a single dog, tongue lolling, panting hard, as it races past you with its nose to the ground.

On one of these days, having seen the tell-tale sign of a fluorescent orange jacket that signalled a hunter was at the end of a track, I started to sing. I was on the lane only a few hundred yards from home and had no intention of taking a detour. My song wasn't terribly exciting, just a few la-la's so that they would know I was there and might realise that I wasn't worth shooting. Over time I made up my own lyrics, my French hunting song, sharing my very low opinion of how they spent their weekends.

On another occasion, walking on a blissfully quiet and peaceful day, I stopped to listen to a robin singing its heart out on a branch above my head, marvelling that such a tiny creature could project its song so far and wide. It occurred to me that when I sang I did it rather timidly, as if it was some sort of apology. That little bird felt no such inhibitions and, the more I thought about it, neither should I. And so I began to sing, picking a song that suited my mood, tentatively increasing the volume until I, like the robin, was singing at the top of my voice, filling my lungs full of air and feeling my heart soar for the pure joy of it.

Either singing or listening to songs is an inherent part of being human, one of the better things about us. It's a rare person who is not moved by a haunting melody or stirred by lyrics, both happy and sad. Singing is good for our health as well, getting more oxygen into our blood, increasing our lung capacity and releasing the 'happy' endorphins. This book is all about finding wonder in our everyday lives, taking pleasure in the smallest of things that are easily accessible to all of us. We can all sing, and there is no need to judge ourselves if we're unlikely to win a talent show. I daresay the birds won't hold it against us.

If you were to meet me one day, walking down a lane and singing at the top of my voice, you might think me eccentric, and perhaps I am. But if ever you find yourself alone in a field, why don't you try singing a verse of your favourite song. Just make sure you sing as loud as you can – you might be surprised at how good it feels.

Something stirs in the woods

Midnight, and something was stirring in the woods above our home. Beneath the stark branches of the tree canopy the world was washed in shades of black and grey, but one of the shadows was on the move, a ghost following the faintest of trails, one that snaked its way past tree trunks and skirted round the dense undergrowth. The shadowy outline disappeared behind a pile of fallen wood, reappeared for a second and then was hidden once more. I wondered if my eyes were playing tricks, straining against the darkness, but suddenly he was there again. It was a fox, his eyes reflected like headlamps. He boldly held the gaze for a second and then he was gone.

He had been captured on our trail camera, which we had strapped to a tree on what we hoped, correctly as it turned out, was a well-frequented animal trail. We left it there for two weeks, long enough for the wildlife to get used to it, and then brought the SD card down and plugged it into the laptop to see what we would find. There were 96 pictures on it. Some of these were close-ups of Michael's hands as he fiddled around to extract the SD card, whilst others were blank as whatever had triggered the camera had long gone by the time the shot was taken, but with that many pictures we had high hopes of seeing a good selection of animals.

I had always assumed seeing animals in the heart of their

wild spaces, particularly in the dark of night, to be the domain of professional photographers, the wildlife documentary makers. However, trail cameras with an infra-red capacity for night-time shots are surprisingly affordable, and to my mind this is a worthwhile expenditure for a device that holds the key to another world. I know it's a wonderful thing to see animals from far-off places, but, for my own part, I have found it far more satisfying to collect my own records of the rather less exotic, but no less thrilling, animals that share my corner of the world. More than that, as the years have passed, it has provided us with an ongoing census of the number and types of animals that take refuge in the woods that surround us. Each year it feels like we meet old friends and breathe a sigh of relief to know that they are still there.

You can gain an insight into the character of a wild animal from the way that it reacts to something alien, like a trail camera, being introduced to its territory. Take the fox, for example. From our first encounter with him, he lived up to his reputation for being canny. He, or she, knew immediately that the camera was there, looking directly at it, ears pricked, intensely alert, and you could sense that he was deciding whether he should be concerned about this strange box attached to a tree. The night-time shots are always captured in black and white, but we also saw him during daylight, his pelt a rich auburn, his tail thick and bushy, with a black-button nose below amber eyes.

The fox tended to keep his distance, unlike the deer who, in the past, have come so close to the camera that the whole screen was filled with their nostrils as they sniffed curiously at this intruder on their patch. On this occasion we only caught a view of the rump of a lone female deer, the distinctive white markings giving her away on a misty morning. We mostly saw the rear end of the badger too as he plodded past in the darkness, but just once he turned and treated us to a headshot, that distinctive black stripe transporting me back into *Wind in the Willows* and the world of Mole, Badger and friends.

The wild boar is primarily a nocturnal creature and, like the badger, he showed no obvious interest in, or awareness of, the camera. We've seen wild boar with our own eyes out in the fields occasionally and spotted one in our field just the once, at twilight, but each time they seem to be creatures with a purpose, with a destination in mind, and they pay little obvious heed to what is around them. Certainly both the deer and fox often pause, heads up, ears swivelling, smelling and listening, ready to flee if necessary. The wild boar keeps moving doggedly on, and no-one gets in his way. Most of our shots of the boar were of the side of his body as he passed by during the night, so close we could see the individual bristles of his coat, but we were fortunate enough to get one close-up in daylight hours. It was just his head but the detail was clear and we noted the texture of his snout. The way it wrinkled reminded me of an elephant's trunk, obviously a foreshortened version, so strong and yet so sensitive.

A few of our medley of pictures were taken up by domestic animals, a pair of hunting dogs, an unwelcome reminder that safety is an illusion. Even less welcome were a few pictures of the hunters, *les chasseurs*, as they scouted through the woods looking for trails. Given the height of the camera we never saw their faces, often just a pair of legs, perhaps a hand holding a wooden stick. The hunting tradition is still very strong in rural France and during the winter season there will always be someone, somewhere, out in the woods and fields with a gun in his hand. As long as humans are around, there is no truly safe haven for the creatures who live in these valleys.

The fact that a small camera can capture such a wide range of pictures is something that we take for granted today but it hasn't always been so easy. In the 1800s photographs had to be developed while the emulsion was still damp. A nature enthusiast had to carry portable darkrooms out in the field, as well as the necessary chemicals and cumbersome glass plates. Subjects were initially limited to stationary objects, plants and landscapes, whilst pictures of animals tended to be domestic as there was a better chance they might stand still long enough for the required exposure time.

One of the first pictures of a wild animal was taken in 1852 by a man called John Dillwyn Llewelyn. He took a picture of a red deer stag with a magnificent set of antlers in a woodland setting, a feat which greatly impressed me until I learned that the animal was dead. It had been stuffed and placed in the woods specifically for the picture, proof of how the camera can lie, even all those years ago.

By the late 1800s a fast shutter had been invented and this opened the door to taking pictures of moving animals. In 1926 Frederick Walter Champion claimed the first picture of a genuinely wild tiger, the image captured as the animal activated a trip wire. The photographer Eric Hoskins embraced the revolutionary new flash technology in the following decade but at a personal cost. He climbed into his hide at night to take pictures of a tawny owl but hadn't realised that the bird had returned to its nest. It attacked him and he lost an eye as a result.

We didn't need to rely solely on our trail camera to know that we had a diversity of life in our woods. If we kept our eyes open as we walked along the track through our field we could spot areas where squirrels had been looking for acorns, or smell the distinctive droppings of a fox. The wild boar, single-minded as ever, felt no need to hide where it had been, regularly turning the grass over in search of something tasty to eat.

Knowing that these animals are in such close proximity evokes strong emotions in me. It gives me a sense of rightness, a conviction that this is how I am supposed to live, in close harmony with nature. Without fail it fills me with quiet delight to see the family group of deer, three adults and two young ones, who often browse in our field as twilight falls, tempered by a fearful despair and anger as I hear the crack of gunshot echoing down the valley on hunt days. As I lie in bed at night, on the cusp of sleep, I like to think that as my day ends, so the nocturnal creatures of the woods have the whole night ahead of them. And lastly, I am thankful, because I know how lucky I am to live in a place where these animals, although threatened, can still roam freely.

MARCH

The air softens and daffodils bloom under a

Lenten moon

The language of the badger

It was night time and we were walking back home after dinner at a friend's house in the village a mile away from home. The moon was up, giving us just enough light to walk without a torch. At one point the lane cuts through a woodland, a high bank on one side and steeply dropping off down the hill on the other. This feels a dark space even in daylight, and at night the trees arch high over our heads and block out the moonlight. I could feel my eyes straining to adjust to a deeper shade of black and then ahead of me there was a flash of white. I blinked and it was gone, then back again, but it seemed disembodied, almost as if it was floating in the darkness. I realised I was looking at a badger, ambling down the middle of the road ahead of us.

Every now and then it turned its head from one side to another, and I could see the broad white stripe running down its snout. We stood still, wondering if it knew we were there, but if so it seemed remarkably unconcerned. A moment later it turned off the road and disappeared into the undergrowth. If we had been here a few minutes earlier or later the chances are that it would never have crossed our path.

The woodlands around us stretch for miles, a patchwork of small parcels of private land belonging to various farmers and landowners. Footpaths are few and it makes a wonderful place for the wildlife to hide away. Despite this we see the deer here regularly, their well-used tracks an obvious sign of their network of trails, and we often walk back to find our grassy track in the field has been turned over by the wild boar, but this was the first time we had seen a badger here with our own eyes and not from our trail camera.

Badgers are an ancient breed. The earliest traces have been dated back three-quarters to half a million years ago, and at times they would have shared their territory with wolves and brown bears. They are nocturnal creatures, rarely seen in daylight hours, more comfortable in the blackness of the night and the silence that falls as we humans retreat inside our homes. Their diet is varied, slugs and soft fruits, even the odd hedgehog if food is scarce, but most of their food comes from earthworms and they can consume as many as 200 in one night.

As we continued on our journey home I wondered where our badger was going. Did it have a family hidden deep in the woods and how did they communicate with each other?

Badger watching of necessity takes place at night when it is difficult to see what the badgers are doing. To help understand their behaviour researchers have recorded the sounds they hear in great detail, analysing the pitch and tone, and matching them with actions. From their work they have compiled a list of at least 16 identifiable sounds which, like any language, are used in different contexts and combinations but together form a unique system of communication. This is the language of the badger and apparently they have much to say.

Young badgers can wail or squeak in distress at being separated from their mothers, and when playing they communicate with each other through a series of bird-like sounds, similar to coos and clucks. The female badger uses a deep purr to warn her young to stay close, resorting to a sharp bark if they become too unruly and need to know who's boss. There are specific sounds to deal with defensive or aggressive situations, beginning with a hiss, a sharp, cat-like sound, and building up to a snarl, which almost always precedes an attack. A female might yelp during mating or bark if she is being annoyed by another adult. If taken by surprise a badger will snort, in much the same way as we might.

Knowing about these sounds and their meaning gave me a new insight into how these wild and ancient animals communicate with each other. Yet again one question led to another and I tried to imagine what their homes were like. They live in setts, or dens, in groups known as clans, typically around four to eight animals of mixed sex. Badgers think big. Their homes can range from 20m to 100m in length with up to 50 entrances and can take years to build. They are meticulously clean, refreshing their bedding of grass, moss and leaves every few days. As we pass our homes on to future generations, so do they. As we add extensions and refit our homes, so do they, each clan maintaining and modifying the structure as they please.

It's too easy to assume that other creatures are somehow less than us, less able to communicate, less intelligent, less complex, but with each month that passes and with each new question that pops into my mind I am learning that this is not the case. So many creatures, large and small, are more sophisticated than I had given them credit for. My eyes have been opened to a new reality and now, every day, nature amazes me.

Spring is in the air

Having spent most of my life in England and Wales I have noticed that spring arrives earlier now that my home is in the south west of France. This is in part simply due to the fact that it is further south, but in fact spring is arriving earlier across the northern hemisphere as a whole. Analysis of 50 years' worth of satellite observations indicates that winters are getting shorter, and that both spring and autumn respectively are becoming longer by on average 15 days. Seasonal patterns that have been dependable and steady for centuries are being affected by climate change, and although we humans may personally rejoice at the promise of shorter winters, this change has worrying implications for plants, birds and insects, who run the risk of falling out of step with the delicate balance of pollination, food and growth cycles.

Spring is officially marked by the spring equinox, which falls on either the 19th, 20th or 21st of March depending on the precise year, but we don't need to be experts to recognise the signs of spring arriving. Regardless of that fixed calendar date, on some instinctive level it is human nature to be aware of an indefinable shift in the air. Now is the time to keep not just our eyes but each of our senses alert to the subtle changes taking place all around us. And there are so many of them: warmer temperatures and longer days, spring lambs and daffodils, bluebells and frogspawn, cherry blossom and birdsong, daisies and dandelions. We shouldn't forget the smell of cut grass, the buds on trees, celandines, butterflies and the first call of the cuckoo. Boxing hares in the fields and hedgehogs coming out of hibernation. Swallows swooping and woodpeckers drumming. Once you start listing out all the wonderful things about spring it's hard to stop.

If we had to pick just one favourite sign of spring I suspect for many of us it would be the birdsong and I have often wondered how such small creatures manage to make so much noise. It comes down to clever design.

Whilst we have a larynx, birds have a syrinx. It reaches lower in their bodies than our larynx, providing a more powerful sound, and is further amplified by an air sac that surrounds it. This combination is so effective that almost 100% of the air that passes through the syrinx is used to produce birdsong, compared to just 2% from our much bigger but less efficient bodies. Somewhat surprisingly, their beaks have little to do with the volume of sound and some birds can sing with their beaks full or even closed.

Bigger birds can make even more noise. At this time of year we are visited by the grey cranes, flying overhead in large numbers as they migrate north from their winter resting sites in Spain. I usually hear them before I see them, a constant chatter in the skies. They tend to fly in loose V formations, the outline constantly changing. Tipping my head back and squinting hard, I can see that every now and then the lead bird falls back, and another takes its place, sharing the load. Their incessant calling is how they communicate, keeping family groups together and warning of danger. They fly at heights of up to 1,500 metres and yet their call is loud and clear to me, so far away back down on the ground. As with the smaller birds, the sound is cleverly amplified.

Given their long necks it is no surprise to find that their tracheas are correspondingly long, coiling their way down into the lungs and attaching themselves onto the sternum. The lungs act like an auditorium, amplifying the vibrations and producing the trumpeting sounds.

All of these familiar signs of spring are a constant in a rapidly changing world, an anchor to hold us steady at a time when so much that we thought unchangeable and indomitable is under threat. As long as I can hear a blackbird sing, smell the bluebells and watch an endearingly fluffy bumblebee bury its head in a daffodil I am reassured that at least some parts of the natural world are still holding strong, still following their seasonal patterns even if the timelines are indeed beginning to change. All around me life is pulsating, pushing forth, singing, buzzing, soaring, calling and filling my senses. If ever there is a time to appreciate what we have, and to feel the joy of simply being alive in our wonderful world, then surely this is it.

Buzz

When we first moved to Le Shack I was astonished by the constant noise and movement of buzzing insects. I have lived in rural landscapes for most of my life, but never have I seen or heard as many insects as I do here. Over time I have learnt to identify the species before I even see them, the helicopter-whirr of the hoverfly, the rumble of the solitary carpenter bee, and deepest of all, the unmistakable bass tone of the hornets, or *frelons*, to give them their French name. At first I had felt slightly uneasy at this constant buzzing, particularly from the hornets who obviously had a nest in the woods somewhere, but I have grown accustomed to them and now they are a vital part of the soundtrack of the countryside, humming gently on the edge of my subconscious. I would miss them if they weren't there.

But why do bees and wasps buzz? One fine spring day I watched a plump bumblebee coming in to land on a clump of daffodils outside the kitchen window and wondered where all that noise came from. Apparently I was hearing the vibrations from the air that they displace with their wings as they fly. The bigger the size of the insect, the slower the number of beats which in turn lowers the pitch of the buzz. My chunky bumblebee beats its wings at 130 per second, whilst the smaller honeybee is faster, reaching approximately 230 beats per second. Having discovered that hornets come in at 100 beats I can now understand why they sound so different, emitting a much deeper rumble.

My bee moved on to a different bloom and as my mind tried to assimilate the astonishing speed at which it was beating its wings, its body wriggled around inside the flower and the tone of its buzz changed. This is known as buzz pollination. The bee is vibrating its flight muscles within its thorax to make that particular noise because certain flowers will only release their pollen for a specific vibration frequency.

In fact that buzzing noise is much more than a side-effect of flying. They use it to communicate, varying the intensity and duration to pass on information about the location of a food source, or as a warning. The queen bee employs a particular pattern of sound to assert her dominance over the colony. They can even use their wings to control body temperature, using them like a fan on hot days to cool down, and warming themselves up with the activity on cold days.

Bees are such busy little things, always on the move, and they remind me that I too have a lot of things to do today and shouldn't have allowed myself to be so easily distracted. Reluctantly, I tear myself away, silently promising that I'll be back once the chores are done.

Cuckoo's boots

Our garden is full of cuckoo's boots. There were a few planted close to the cabin when we arrived but I have lifted them each year and spread them and now we have a fine spring display, swathes of soft lilac that soothe the eye and a sweet scent that drifts gently on the breeze. You might know them by their Latin name, *Hyacinthoides hispanica*, or most likely by their common name of Spanish bluebells, but they have a host of other traditional names: witches' thimbles, lady's nightcap, fairy flower, wild hyacinth. Scotland provides a few choice names of its own with *cra'-tae*, or crow's toes, which is baffling as I can see nothing crow-like in a bluebell flower or, my personal favourite, *gowk's thummies* which means cuckoo's thimbles. Cuckoos are primarily known for their poor parenting habits rather than their sewing skills but it conjures up a rather delightful image none the less. There is also the intriguing name of *granfer griggles*, the first half of the phrase being an old word for grandfather and the second either referring to old apples on a tree or a lively young person. Apparently the latter explanation is preferred and has been extrapolated to suggest young children happily running around their grandfather's woods.

Today we value these beautiful flowers for their colour and their scent but in the Bronze Age the sap was used as a glue to fix feathers onto arrows and during the Elizabethan period the bulbs were crushed to make starch for the ruffs of collars and sleeves. Our ancestors were adept at using the resources they had to hand for their day-to-day needs, much of it based on plant-lore. If I need glue I pop along to my local DIY store, not as time-consuming but much less of an achievement.

In the language of flowers, the bluebell is a symbol of everlasting love. Apparently, if you can turn the flower inside out without tearing it you will win the heart of the one you love. I can't imagine who dreamed up this idea but I sacrificed one of my precious flowers to see if it could be done. Not surprisingly, given how delicate they are, I failed in my task but my husband assures me he still loves me, so all is not lost.

Heady scents

Most of us use our eyes as our primary guide, our default setting for processing what is happening around us, but in springtime it seems as if the other senses jostle for that pole position, proclaiming that there is so much to smell, to hear, or to feel and that our experience of the joys of this particular season will barely scratch the surface without them to guide us deeper into it.

I have an emotional reaction to many of the sensual pleasures of springtime. There is something evocative about the smell of cut grass, a promise of fine weather and a long summer being outdoors. I almost swoon at times at the delicate scent of a lilac flower or a rose, a very different reaction from Michael who wrinkles his nose and proclaims it as 'sickly'. I am so beguiled by the positive associations that I have for these particular smells that I never think about the actual mechanics of why they smell and how I recognise them.

But how do we smell? Each time we breathe, tiny molecules that are constantly in the air around us are drawn into our nasal cavity. If you have ever doubted that the air is saturated with these particles just give a jumper or a bed sheet a shake when the sun is shining through and you will see how many tiny motes of dust suddenly appear. Whilst I am swept up in the romance of smelling the roses, the brain is clinically analysing chemicals: hydrogen, oxygen, nitrogen, dust or pollen. These chemicals attach themselves to tiny, hair-like attachments in our nose called 'cilia' which begin the process of sending sensory information to the brain. It will then match that information to data in our memory banks and send back the information that allows us to recognise and understand what we are smelling. If the chemicals do not find a match our brain will call on another sense, like sight or taste, to build up a more detailed picture so that it can imprint this new experience into our mind.

Armed with this new insight, I went into the garden and pressed my nose into a bunch of daffodils. Instead of just enjoying it I tried to concentrate on the mechanics of what I was doing, to see if I had any awareness of all that detective work being done by my brain. There was nothing. It all happened too quickly, too automatically for me to be aware of it. Thinking about it, I realised I preferred it that way. The brain could concentrate on chemical analysis; I was happy to close my eyes and just breathe in that heady scent.

APRIL

April showers and wild flowers

The art of pond watching

There is an art to pond watching. At first glance it seems as if nothing is going on, but it requires patience. Our pond is only a small one, probably no more than nine feet in diameter, with an area of decking to one side that is big enough for a bench. I like to think of it as the heart of the garden, in much the same way as a woodburner makes the house a home. We spend a lot of time sitting by that pond, whether it's for our morning coffee, for a breather after a session doing battle with bracken or brambles, or as a place to relax with a glass of wine when all the work is done. It draws us back for the final visit of the day when we sit in contented silence and watch the sun go down.

It may be a small pond but it is full of life and I know that, given enough time, something will swim or float into my line of sight. Where I position myself will determine how much satisfaction I gain from the experience. My preferred location is to come down to ground level, lying fully stretched out on my front, my chin propped on my hands, as close to the edge of the decking as I can go, a perfect place from which to gaze into the depths. From this vantage point I come closer to sharing the perspective of the various creatures that live in and around the water.

After five minutes or so, I find that I have tuned in to the way that the newts tuck themselves underneath the pond weed, or I'll recognise the flash of movement out of the corner of my eye as a boatman scuttles over the surface. What looks like a rotting leaf will shift slightly and I suddenly realise that I have been looking at a toad for the past ten minutes without being aware of it. After another ten minutes a salamander floats into view and lingers for a moment in the shallows, its body a nondescript mottled green and brown but its feet intricately striped, and I smile as I imagine that it is wearing designer boots or gloves. All of these other-worldly creatures seem to take life very slowly, being still for long periods of time, doing nothing, although when they are disturbed they move so quickly, gone in an instant. From my limited experience most creatures spend long periods of time doing not much; it is only we humans who rush around all day long.

I grimace at the crick in my neck. I've been here too long. As a typical human I have many things I am supposed to be doing, a list of must-do, should-do and might-do, but I really don't care. This is a far better use of my time. A lizard darts out from under a nearby stone, lifts it head and stares at me with a cold, reptilian eye. I stare back at it, feeling like Gerald Durrell in *My Family and Other Animals.* What a childhood he had, and how I envied his ability to lose not just hours but days watching the minutiae of life around him, completely engrossed and forgetful of the humdrum chores of life. I'm 63 years old and this pond is teaching me to be a child again, a crash course in how to live completely in the moment.

I wonder whether I need to know the precise names of the creatures I am looking at, what species they belong to, how they breed or how long they live. I usually love to learn new things but today my heart sinks at the thought of sitting in front of a screen. I suspect it will spoil the moment, diminish the experience rather than add to it. It's enough for me just to be here, watching them.

As if to reward my decision a young grass snake slithers into view, side-winding its way through the water with sinuous grace. I turn over, close my eyes and feel the sun on my face. Perhaps I'll stay a little longer...

The dance of the butterflies

There is a thin line between love and war. It's true of humans and also for animals, birds and insects. As I walked along the track in our field one morning a pair of lemon-yellow butterflies launched themselves from the grass in front of me. They were spiralling energetically around each other but I was unsure as to whether they were two males seeing each other off, or whether it was a courtship dance. There was a gentleness to their movements and I decided that this was more likely to be a prelude to mating. When the males fight they hold nothing back, throwing themselves at each other, using their bodies as weapons in the absence of having anything else they can call on, uncaring of how fragile those bodies are. Like all of us, once the hormones are raging common sense goes out of the window.

In the butterfly world it is the female who has the final say when it comes down to choosing a partner and the males have to work for the privilege. Some males will pick a good vantage spot and keep watch for a female whilst others are more proactive and will patrol their territory. The male performs a dance to convince the female that he is a worthy suitor but his flapping wings aren't just for show. They release pheromones which will hopefully go in her direction and not be lost on the breeze. If the dance is good enough and the pheromones do their job she will signal her acceptance by changing her stance and they will mate by joining together at their abdomens. The female lays fertilised eggs in the ground where they will hatch as caterpillars, which will eventually become butterflies, and the cycle begins once more.

By the time the eggs hatch both parents may well be dead. Some butterflies have a lifespan of no more than one or two weeks. They shine so brightly, one of nature's beautiful creatures, but not for long. Who knows if they are aware that their time is limited, but their sole purpose and drive is taken up by reproducing. It is not in their remit to question whether there is any point to such a life, no time to ponder on how these cycles turn and turn again, year after year, millions of butterflies hatching, breeding and dying in a few short weeks. I wonder how differently our human lives would be if all we had was a few weeks, but actually the answer should be the same regardless of the amount of time allotted to us. We can learn from the butterflies, not necessarily by indulging in a fortnight of unbridled sex, but we can choose to live our lives with passion, with intensity, making the most of every day.

Legacy

A big oak stands like a sentinel by our front gate. If I stretch my arms around its girth I can't bring my fingertips together. It's only half the tree it used to be, literally, as at some time long before we arrived half of it came down and now all the growth, and all the considerable weight, is on one side only. Michael has leaned a ladder up against it and peered down into the open cavity of the trunk, completely hollow, a funnel for leaves to gather, and a desirable residence for hornets, although they have only used it for one season since we have been here.

Each year we look at this tree and discuss whether we should have it taken down by a tree surgeon in a controlled manner before it falls down in a gale and completely blocks the road. Each year we convince ourselves that what remains is a healthy tree, and that oaks can survive for years with a hollow trunk.

Cutting down a tree this old simply feels wrong. And the fact that it is an oak tree makes the decision even harder. The oak is known as the king of trees for good reasons, providing a place to eat, shelter and breed for over 2,300 species. Its flowers and leaves nurture squirrels, moths, bees, birds and spiders, aphids and wood ants. The acorns are a food source for badgers, wild boar, mice, woodpeckers and blue jays. The roots provide a habitat for fungi and the branches for lichens, mosses and liverworts.

Even after they die oak trees continue to offer refuge and succour to the creatures that live on and around them.

Deadwood is softer than living wood, easier for birds like woodpeckers to make their nests in, and a perfect home for bats, owls and squirrels, but more than this it is the lifeblood of a woodland. As the tree decays its nutrients are released back into the soil, enriching it and ensuring a fertile growing medium for new trees. I think it must be wonderful to leave such a legacy, yet another reason to stand in awe before these beautiful trees.

What legacy would I leave behind? How would my contribution compare to that of the oak? After a few minutes of increasingly desperate pondering I couldn't think of anything. I had always thought I would be cremated when I died, but perhaps I need to rethink that one. At least with a woodland burial the worms would be glad of me.

Albert Einstein stated that energy cannot be destroyed, only changed into other forms. Our bodies are recycled when we are buried. As we break down into our constituent parts we become part of the soil, food for plants which in turn becomes food for animals and so, in a sense, this is a form of legacy and we are still part of the universe. Even in cremation all is not completely lost as some of our atoms are released directly into the atmosphere and so become part of another of the Earth's systems.

Does it matter if we don't leave anything behind, other than our memory in the hearts of our loved ones? After all, not everyone is a famous scientist or painter or inventor. I am not a religious person and tend towards the belief that once I am gone, I am gone. However there is some good I can do while I am here, just as the oak does. My contribution is not going to change the world, but in a small way it might make it a better place. I can leave saplings to grow strong rather than cut back and tidy as is our human compulsion. I can choose plants for the bees as well as for myself, and this particular thought lead to another. With a new purpose I looked at where we had left a young plantation of oak to grow and could see how they would be perfect partners for Spanish bluebells in the spring. I looked at the track and envisaged how it would look if it was planted with daffodils along its entire length. This could be my labour of love for the land, each year lifting and spreading our stock of bluebells, each autumn buying in a sack or two of daffodils, our reward not just the sheer beauty of it but also the satisfaction of knowing that these plants are much loved by the bees and other pollinators and that they will continue to grow and spread long after we are gone.

Singing a sunrise

After a long winter the natural world is casting off the shackles and suddenly it seems as if the canvas has been painted green. Green is spring's favourite colour, a sign of new life, of energy and revival, but one simple word cannot begin to describe this explosion of growth, so lush and so rich. As I cycle along the lanes in the woods near my home I see shades of emerald and jade, hues of lime and moss, bright fresh greens contrasting with darker earthy tones.

It's early in the morning and the air is filled with birdsong. Occasionally I will catch a glimpse of movement in the branches, a flash of a wing in flight, but for the most part the birds are hidden from view. Perhaps it is the fact that I can hear them more clearly than see them which gives me the impression of being encircled by a choir of feathered songsters, blackbirds, thrushes and robins, blue tits and chaffinches, each bird filling their tiny lungs and singing as if this is the last day of their lives. They trill and twitter, warble and whistle, chirp and croon, uncaring of whether they sing in harmony, their sole aim to be the star of the show. Their joy is infectious and I can feel my heart swelling in response.

These woods are mostly oak but occasionally there is a plantation of pines where the scent is strong, clean and wholesome, and I take a deep breath. The sun is slowly rising, and as it gets higher it breaks through open gaps in the canopy, fingertips of soft light filtering between the leaves and branches, stripes of light and shadow across the tarmac. Outlines of solid tree trunks become hazy and insubstantial in the mist from the early morning dew and the woods shimmer with mystery. And still all around me the birds sing, singing themselves a sunrise, for who can resist their melody? Certainly not the sun, for with every minute that passes he is lured deeper into the woods, the cold shadows fleeing before him.

I am grateful for the light. It's a new dawn. A new day. And all is right in the world.

Mary-Jane Houlton

MAY

The world turns green, such a sight to be seen

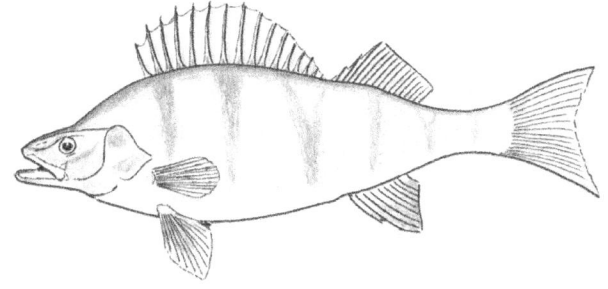

Fishy feelings

It's May 1st and our first day back in the water. For the last seven years we have spent our summers exploring European rivers and canals on our motor cruiser, *Olivia Rose*. We've covered most of France, parts of Belgium, Luxembourg and Germany but we will be spending this season in the Netherlands.

It is a distance of around 1,200km from Le Shack to the boatyard in the Netherlands where *Olivia Rose* spent the previous winter and the journey takes us two days. We board the night train to Paris from Tarbes in the south west of France, make our way across the city early the next morning for the Eurostar to Rotterdam, then catch another train to Gorinchem and finally hop onto a bus which drops us off within walking distance of the boatyard.

It might seem a long and convoluted journey, especially when compared to flying, but it gives me time to adjust, mentally and emotionally rather than physically, to living quite a different lifestyle for the next four months. Le Shack is a tiny home but, as you might expect, a boat is even smaller, although it's still a comfortable space to live in and satisfies all our needs. We move on most days, perhaps stopping for a night or two if something appeals, but this is a nomadic lifestyle and our view is continually changing. We go where the river or canal takes us, rarely planning more than a day or two ahead, and although we have an idea of what we want to do for the next few months it is a loose one and tends to evolve each week. I am looking forward to seeing how my questions develop as our days adjust to this new order.

We share this watery world with other boaters, with walkers and cyclists along the footpaths and cycle tracks, and also with fishermen. The fishermen rarely seem to catch anything but when they do it is usually returned to the water, occasionally measured and photographed first if it is a big one. I can understand catching a single fish to eat it but have never really understood the fascination of fishing as a sport. My sympathies have always rested with the fish, although I have assumed that they have little capacity to think or to feel and so the experience of being pulled out of the water with a hook stuck in the side of their mouths might not be as horrible as it looks.

By chance we happened to pass a fisherman one day just as he was landing a sizeable fish, around 18 inches long. It thrashed around for a few moments while he struggled to remove the hook and then he put it back in the water. Afterwards I found myself questioning my previous assumptions. How could that not have been a painful, stressful experience for the fish? What level of intelligence do they possess? What sort of lives do they live down there in the murky depths where we can't see them?

It turned out that my previous assumptions were distressingly wrong. They may not feel pain exactly as we do, and their expressionless faces make it hard to read what they are feeling and therefore easier to convince ourselves that they are unaffected, but the science is very clear. They have pain receptors in their mouths which means that being caught on a hook and line is just as horrible an experience for them as it looks. They also need water to breathe, and the more time they spend out of the water the greater the level of stress. As we might panic and thrash around in the water if we were drowning, so the fish is thrashing around on the bank because it is drowning in air.

It has long been argued that they lack the higher brain functions and have no memory but further research has found evidence that they are social and affectionate animals, although not all fish are created equal and so these attributes vary from species to species. They can communicate through sounds, scents, electric pulses and motions. For example, the red gurnard fish, which can be found around UK waters as well as the Mediterranean Sea, contracts its swim bladder to create vibrations that produce a range of sounds. Collectively known as sea robins, these are chatty fish, emitting grunts throughout the day, whilst cod, in contrast, are generally quieter fish except when spawning. The Australian elephant fish use electric signals to identify each other and pass on information, such as age, size, how far away they are from each other, and whether they are male or female.

Certain species of fish can also recognise each other and remember past social interactions. A researcher played a particular song whilst feeding fish in captivity. They were released into the wild and five months later that song was played out at sea. The fish recognised the sound, associated it with food and returned.

I have been continually surprised at the answers to many of my questions during this year, and for the most part also enchanted and intrigued at what I have learnt. However this particular topic leaves me with mixed feelings. I can wonder at the hidden lives of fish, but the supposedly gentle art of fishing has a darker side. My previously rather vague sympathy for the fish has strengthened and I now feel a sense of dread when we pass a fisherman reeling in his catch. The fact that it seems to be a rare occurrence is no consolation.

What lies beneath?

The Keukenhof Gardens in the Netherlands are the largest flower gardens in Europe. Each year around seven million tulip bulbs are planted on the 32-hectare site, and just under one and a half million tourists come to visit for the few weeks that the gardens are open. This year my husband and I joined the throng, walking through the gates and instantly becoming lost in the tide of humanity that swept along the paths. The pace slowed slightly as we all jostled our way through the display pavilions, hit a traffic jam around the ice-cream sellers and food halls, and then picked up speed again as paths meandered through woods and around borders.

The gardens were magnificent. It was as if someone had decided to play a game of bowls with pots of paint of all colours, rolling them out along the ground, the paint spilling out in distinct themes of pink and red, lilac and purple, white and yellow. In other areas they had dispensed with such discipline, jumbling up every colour that you could ever name, flamboyant, exuberant, dazzling.

Despite the constant chatter and the pressure of people all around me, I still found these gardens beautiful. I love flowers and had naively assumed that this motivation would be a common factor amongst other visitors but at one point I stopped looking at the tulips and began to observe my fellow man. It soon became apparent that for some of them today was primarily an exercise in taking a selfie and sharing it on social media. I also heard the odd grumble about some of the tulips being past their best, as if the flowers should be like plastic copies you could buy in the gift shops here, everlasting rather than something that was obviously going to die and go over at some point during the time the gardens were open. It is an inevitable part of the natural process, something to be accepted rather than criticised, and the gardeners had worked hard to ensure that, as one area began to fade, another would come to a peak to replace it.

I left my fellow human beings to their selfies and turned my attention back to the tulips. Their glory is short-lived; they blossom for a few weeks each year and once their foliage has died away they disappear completely, leaving no clue that they have ever been. On this cloudy spring day they seemed like a miracle, brash and blowsy, or soft and delicate depending on which direction you looked, but then I began to question where they came from, to wonder about the role of the bulb itself, and perhaps that is where the true miracle begins.

Over the winter months the plant appears dormant, invisible to our eye, but beneath the soil it is only half-asleep. As temperatures fall and the daylight hours grow shorter a stopwatch is triggered within the bulb. After so many weeks at a certain level of coolness, hormones activate a new growth cycle and the same factors that sent it to sleep back in the beginning of winter now shift into reverse and wake it up. The days become longer, the temperatures warmer and the carbohydrates stored in the bulb are turned into sugar, providing the energy for the leaves and flowers to push up out of the bulb and into the air.

Words like hormones, sugars and carbohydrates apply to humans just as much as plants. The way we live is also affected by warmth and light, all of which would intimate that we have something in common with all of the many plants that we both gain so much pleasure from and also rely upon to ensure our ecosystems can function. And yet it is so easy to think of them as completely separate, their needs quite different to ours.

I assumed that my lasting memory of my visit to Keukenhof would be the splendour of the tulips and indeed it is, but I now have a far greater appreciation of the bulb as well as the flower, modest, unassuming and hidden. The bulb and the flower are two halves that make the whole, one grabbing all the attention and the other doing most of the work. You can't have one without the other.

Fending for ourselves

We were moored up next to a wide expanse of grass, a perfect picnic spot for the local people on a sunny day. I watched as a young couple played with their newborn son as he lay on a blanket. He was a happy youngster, chortling with delight as his parents tickled his tummy, rolling around on the rug but quite incapable of sitting up without help. It would be around 10 to 18 months before he would start walking and many more years before he could live and fend for himself.

On the river new life was appearing all around us, coots, grebes and moorhens, geese and ducks, all busy making nests, sitting on eggs and then feeding and caring for their young with varying degrees of devotion. Greater crested grebes would paddle past us with their chicks perched on their backs. This easy life lasts no more than three weeks, after which the parent flips the indignant youngsters into the water, beginning the process where they learn to fend for themselves. They start catching and finding their own food after two months or so and can fly after three to four months.

The chicks of the greylag goose are born 'precocial', which means that they come into the world in an advanced state, able to feed themselves and move independently almost immediately. The adults mate for life and the chicks, fully fledged after just 8–9 weeks, stay within the family group until the following spring, when they have to make way for the next generation of chicks.

This ability to fend for themselves either from birth or soon after is not limited to birds. A newborn lamb, calf, deer or foal is on its feet within moments of its birth. Why is there such a difference between humans and other species? For the first few months of our lives we can't even lift our head up without help. We roll over for the first time at about four months old and take our first steps after 12 months or so. We dominate the world and yet we are helpless for so many of our young years.

It all comes down to the size of our brain. The brains of many animals and birds are almost fully developed when they are born so that they can hit the ground running, sometimes literally. This ability gives them a huge advantage during those first vulnerable days and weeks, not one that we can share. The size of our skull at birth, and therefore our brain, is dictated by the size of the human pelvis. The relatively narrow pelvis that we now have is a product of evolution. Six million years ago we stopped crawling around on all fours and got up on two legs. Our hips gradually became narrower, allowing us to walk longer distances in search of food and to run from predators or aggressors.

Humans are not just born helpless, a state referred to as 'altricial'. We are, in a sense, born prematurely. The next stage of our growth happens outside the mother's body, as our brains grow larger and we learn to walk, talk and think for ourselves. The human brain takes a rather astonishing 20 years to fully develop.

Whilst this extended development might seem to be an initial disadvantage it has benefits. It promotes strong family ties, an interdependence of family and society that makes us strong. What we lose in those early days and years doesn't hold us back in the long term, quite the reverse.

I sat on deck and watched a family of greylag geese paddle serenely past, one adult at the front and the other at the rear, and marvelled at the strength and self-sufficiency of those tiny bodies. And then I looked at my fellow human beings walking past and marvelled at them as well. There is so much we don't know about ourselves and so much we take for granted. All life is astonishing in its complexity and ingenuity. It's no bad idea to step back every now and then and appreciate it.

A nightingale sang

I can remember the first time I heard a nightingale sing. It was during our first year on *Olivia Rose*, in 2017, while we were cruising in northern France. We'd been out for a walk after dinner and as we came back to the boat the nightingale began to sing, a unique combination of whistles, trills and chattering sounds that I'd never heard before. I wasn't looking out for it, and I can't even remember the name of the town we were in, but I do have a vivid picture in my mind of that stretch of footpath and the unruly hedge that bordered it, a perfect hiding place for a small bird, and I can remember that thrill of pleasure as a nightingale serenaded me for the first time.

Ever since then I have made a point of looking out for them or, more accurately, listening out for them. You might think that something that sings so beautifully would also be beautiful, or at least striking, but the nightingale is a rather plain bird, about seven inches long with dull brown plumage and a yellow beak. I heard one the other evening and could tell it was singing in a small copse of trees right in front of me, but I never saw it. I never have seen one. Why do they sing at night, when the majority of birds sing in the daytime?

It is the male who sings and he is trying to attract a mate. These birds migrate from West Africa, arriving in Europe and the UK for the spring breeding season, and so his song is a bid to let the female know she has reached her destination and it is time to come down from the skies and mate with him. This still doesn't adequately explain why he can't sing his song in the daytime with the same effect but I can find no other explanation.

The nightingale is not the only bird to sing at night, and his song is sometimes confused with that of the robin or blackbird, but none of them have the same range. The nightingale can produce 1,000 different sounds, compared to 340 by the skylark and 100 by the blackbird.

During the 19th century they were a collector's item, prized as caged birds so that people could enjoy their song, but few survived captivity. Those that lived through to the autumn often killed themselves, dashed against the bars of their cages as the instinct to migrate was too strong to resist. Few things are as wild and as free as a bird and it seems unbelievably cruel to keep them this way. Thankfully, those days are gone, which is just as well as their numbers are in decline. Now, when I hear a nightingale I know how lucky I am.

Mary-Jane Houlton

JUNE

The lazy, hazy days of summer

Lost for words

It's 7am on the River Eem in the Netherlands and for the first time in days we have woken to still waters with not a breath of wind. It is that magical hour when the world is waiting to see what the day will bring and there is a sense of peace in the stillness. Reeds line the riverbanks and beyond them a grassy patchwork of fields rolls on without interruption until it seemingly drops off the end of the world. The landscape is so utterly lacking in any contour that it is almost two dimensional and it would be easy to revert to the outdated belief that the world is flat. The only sign of human habitation is a single farmhouse in the distance, cows lowing in the barn, with the distant rumble of a tractor to indicate that the farmer is up and about his business.

Above us the sky is a washed-out insipid blue, but banks of creamy white clouds are gathering on the horizon and I know the wind will soon be rising once more. Lifting my gaze, up and up until my neck hurts, I can see only sky and the sheer enormity of it overwhelms me.

It is impossible to spend any length of time cruising through this lowland country without becoming intensely aware of the raw power of the wind and the water. Wayward and capricious, the elements are one minute benign, the next malevolent, and we have learnt that they can be quick to turn.

Today the weather has woken in a good mood, and so we cast off, the bow of *Olivia Rose* slicing cleanly through the calm waters. I can hear the soft *swish-swish* of the water as it parts to let the boat through and, looking back, I can see our wake gently slapping at the banks. A sleeping grebe bobs about to one side of the river, its head tucked neatly beneath its wing, apparently quite unperturbed at our passing, although I catch it just as it blinks open a watchful eye for a second. Standing outside of myself I try to picture how we must look from way on high, imagining that perhaps Zeus, the Greek god of weather, is looking down on two humans on a small boat making their way along a sparkling ribbon of water, an insignificant speck of humanity in this vast watery wonderland. I like to think that he might feel a pang of envy, wishing for a moment that he could come down to our level and feel what I am feeling at this special moment.

But what exactly am I feeling?

The English language is a rich and diverse one. There is no simple answer as to exactly how many words there are but some estimates put it as high as a million, whilst a typical dictionary might hold 300,000 words. It is estimated that the average English speaker could know around 40,000 words, although they actively use only half that number. Despite this treasure chest of words I am struggling to find ones which fully express what I am feeling.

I turn to my thesaurus and start hunting. It suggests words like serenity, gladness, ease, happiness, elation and joy, and these words strike a chord but they don't fully capture my emotions. Perhaps there are some feelings for which there are no words. I abandon my search to define the moment, turn my face up to the sun and close my eyes. It is enough.

How do you measure something you can't see?

I pulled my fleece more tightly around me and looked at the weather forecast on my phone. It was the third time I had checked it that day and it wasn't going to get any better no matter how often I looked at it. It was going to be an extremely windy night and we would need to prepare for it.

I never paid too much attention to the wind until we had *Olivia Rose* but now it is a key part of our lives, particularly in the Netherlands, which is nothing if not a windy country. What might not seem a particularly strong wind when your feet are firmly grounded on land has different implications when you are on the water. We spend our time on inland waters which are, for the most part, less challenging than the open sea but strong winds still pose problems. Boats become difficult to handle, particularly as you slow down to get through locks or wait for a bridge to lift, and also when mooring up. A strong on-shore wind can literally pin a boat to its mooring so that you can't move on until it dies down and in stormy conditions you need to make sure your lines are secure and tie down anything that might blow away.

We pay special attention to the weather forecast during our cruising months, particularly wind speeds, but how do you measure something as ephemeral as the wind? We can't see it and can't contain it. However, we can see how it affects the things that it blows past and around and if we study the way they react we can get a reasonably accurate idea of the force being exerted.

The Beaufort scale, or Beaufort wind force scale as it is officially known, offers a means of evaluating wind power without relying on wind instruments. In 1805 Sir Frances Beaufort devised a table consisting of a series of numbers, or levels, that could be used to estimate the force of the wind and therefore allow sea-going vessels to prepare for it accordingly. Seafarers had recorded weather conditions in their captain's logs for hundreds of years but, not surprisingly, they were subjective, with one man's 'stiff breeze' being another man's 'soft breeze'. Beaufort succeeded in producing a set of parameters which, whilst not based on exact science, could be used with some level of objectivity and understanding by everyone. It was adopted officially by the Royal Navy in the 1930s and is still used to this day, although it has evolved over the years. The scale runs from 0 to 17, although the last five numbers apply to tropical typhoons and are only used in areas around China and Taiwan, so for most of us the more useful part of the table runs from 1 to 12.

The first scale related to the effect of wind on the sails of a frigate, with terminology that was appropriate at the time: for example, a wind that was 'just sufficient to give steerage' to 'that which no canvas sails could withstand'. In 1916, as a result of the growth of steam power, the descriptions changed to reflect how the sea behaved, rather than the sails of a ship, and were also expanded to cover conditions on land. Below is a potted version of the modern scale, familiar to many from the shipping forecasts on BBC Radio 4. The official scale measures the wind in knots, kilometres per hour (kph), miles per hour (mph) and in metres per second, the latter used mainly by meteorologists. All these numbers can be confusing so I have included just the one measurement, miles per hour, in the hope that it will convey something to most people.

Force 0: Calm and still, smoke rises vertically.

Force 1: Light winds at 1–3 mph, slight ripples on the water, smoke drift shows wind direction.

Force 2: Light breeze at 4–7 mph, small wavelets, wind felt on face.

Force 3: Gentle breeze at 8–12 mph, scattered white horses, flag begins to wave.

Force 4: Gentle breeze at 13–18 mph, frequent white horses, raises dust and loose paper, small branches moving.

Force 5: Fresh breeze 19–24 mph, small trees sway, white caps form on inland waters, chance of spray.

Force 6: Strong breeze at 25–31 mph, large waves begin to form, umbrellas hard to use, large branches on trees move, whistling heard in telegraph wires.

Force 7: High wind, moderate gale at 32–38 mph, sea heaps up and white foam breaks from waves, whole trees in motion, walking in wind is difficult.

Force 8: Gale at 39–46 mph, moderately high waves of greater length, twigs and branches break off trees.

Force 9: Strong/severe gale at 47–54 mph, high waves, sea begins to roll, roof tiles blow off buildings.

Force 10: Storm/gale at 55–63 mph, seldom experienced inland but trees will be uprooted, considerable structural damage. Very high waves at sea with long overhanging crests, heavy rolling and limited visibility.

Force 11: Violent storm at 64–72 mph, small and medium-sized ships lost to view for long periods of time behind waves, widespread damage to vegetation and buildings.

Force 12: Hurricane at 73–136 mph, a Category 1 hurricane or tornado, air filled with foam and spray, sea completely white. Devastation.

As a general rule, tables of figures do not make for exciting reading, but the same can't be said of the Beaufort scale. The tension mounts with each level and by the time I am reading about Force 10 I can feel a knot of fear in my stomach. In my mind the waves are like mountains, the ship rising and falling, and each time she drops the sailors must wonder if their end has come. The water pounds the decks, the wind shrieks in the rigging, the timbers groan and then the ship begins to break apart. What had been the sailor's refuge against the elements becomes their coffin, as they lie trapped under falling timbers or are swept into the cold, churning seas. And then that final, chilling word – devastation. What happens next? Will any survive? If that isn't a cliff-hanger I don't know what is.

Searching for a wilderness

The Netherlands is a small, densely populated country and you are never far from a road, houses, people, planes and other boats. Much as I enjoy being here there are times when it feels too manicured, as if all the inherent untidiness of nature has been snipped and cut until it has forgotten the exuberant joy of running wild, and there is always the constant noise and movement of people.

As we travelled north towards Friesland we passed through the Weerribben-Wieden National Park, the largest wetland in north-west Europe. It is a landscape of lakes and narrow waterways pushing their way through reed-lands and swamp forests, much of it only accessible by small boats. Michael and I hired a Canadian canoe and set off on an 8km paddle through the heart of it in search of wilderness and solitude.

As we glided through the water hundreds of dragonflies lifted off from amongst the reeds that lined the channel, blue-black with chunky bodies. Many of them were mating, flying connected tail to head, and it made their flights a little haphazard at times. The water lilies were so close I could reach out my hand and touch them. We could hear birdsong in the trees all around us, and I spotted a warbler perched on a reed. We passed four or five ducks but the coots, grebes and various geese that had been our constant companions on the waterways so far were conspicuous in their absence and I couldn't understand why. At one of the narrowest points we came across a lone swan, who flared its wings and hissed at us but let us pass by without any further sign of aggression.

As time passed we settled into a comfortable rhythm of paddling, the only sound our oars slicing through the water. It was early in the season and we came across just three other boats during our journey. It felt peaceful and serene, a special place indeed, but it didn't feel like a wilderness and this surprised me. Why not? What was missing?

The first four letters of the word hold the clue. A wilderness has to be wild, untamed, uncultivated and free from the influence and management of mankind. It is getting ever harder to find anywhere on this planet which has not been altered by humans but this national park, as natural as it might seem at first glance, has been almost entirely created by us. Originally this area was a land of peat and bog, and the Dutch harvested these natural resources, cutting the peat for fuel and the reeds for roofing. In some areas they dug too deep and created great lakes, and between them channels were cut and cleared as part of the transport network for moving goods around. Today the land would revert to bog and swamp without constant intervention and maintenance, and new waterways are regularly created.

To my mind a true wilderness has an edge to it, a frisson of danger and unpredictability, and you can't help but be acutely aware that it is bigger than us, not something we can control. I realised that this was what was missing here. It had no edge. The human race was still firmly in control, although the role was now one of nurture and support rather than extraction for trade.

Regardless of how it was formed there was no doubt this

was now a haven for wildlife and a green and peaceful environment. It was enough to enjoy it for what it was. Time in the wilderness would have to wait.

Stormy days

It was a day of storms, rolling in one after the other over the space of four or five hours. We were safely moored up on the bank of a sheltered channel, well away from the choppy waters of the nearby lake, and we could see the weather coming in. The skies were charcoal-black, a rainbow arcing in the distance, a sign that someone was already getting wet. The wind whistled through the halyards of the yachts in the marina opposite us and *Olivia Rose* began to rock in the water. There was a crack of thunder and a flicker of movement high in the sky caught my eye. It was a bird, perhaps a crow although it was too far away to be sure, storm-tossed and vulnerable. And then the heavens opened and the rain ricocheted across the water. I wondered why that bird was out in such weather, and then my mind moved on to question what birds do to survive extreme conditions of wet and cold.

They say that forewarned is forearmed, good advice which birds are well placed to take heed of because they read the weather in ways that we cannot. They are able to pick up on 'infrasound', a low frequency noise, that precedes an approaching storm. The perching birds, like jays, sparrows and crows, will find a branch close to the trunk of a tree, picking the lee side where they can take advantage of some protection from the wind or the rain. The choice of tree can be crucial; a dense evergreen is better than the bare branches of a deciduous tree over the winter months, and has the added benefit of keeping the ground below free of snow so that they can more easily forage for food to keep them warm.

Birds that roost in cavities, such as small owls and woodpeckers, can return to their nest. Others can seek refuge in hedges and barns and they will often group together in numbers, relying on their combined body heat to keep them warm.

There are a number of physical aspects that also help them. The anatomy of their feet is such that when they relax, their grip automatically tightens on the branch, allowing them to sleep without falling off. Their spindly legs and tiny feet benefit from 'counter-current circulation' which means they have cold blood in their feet, ensuring very little heat loss when standing on cold or frozen ground. When they sense a change in air pressure, another warning sign, they will fill up on food, instinctively knowing that a warm belly can be a lifesaver. However the biggest thing that works in their favour is their feathers, a downy coat that keeps cold air away and traps body heat.

Bad weather doesn't just affect the birds personally, it can also destroy or damage their habitats. Salt marshes can be flooded, sand dunes blown away and reedbeds flattened, all of which have a long-lasting effect on food supplies and nesting places. In 2013 on the north Norfolk coast a strange sight was seen in the aftermath of a severe storm. Mute swans, and even a grey seal, were seen swimming along the flooded coast road, seemingly unfazed by this altered landscape.

In that same year around 50,000 dead sea birds washed up in west Wales due to winter storms. Whilst land-based birds can more easily find a safe haven in bad weather, sea birds face a tougher challenge, often struggling to find food and becoming progressively weaker. Many more sea birds would have died out at sea during that time, their bodies never to be found.

I sometimes fall into the trap of judging other creatures by my own ability to stay warm and dry, not realising that they can be better equipped to survive than I would be if I didn't have a house, or a boat, to shelter in. Sadly, there are times when the weather takes its toll, and neither their finely-tuned instincts nor the clever design of their bodies is enough to save them. Somehow the loss seems worse because it often goes unseen by us and, in these days of ever more erratic weather due to climate change, we are actively contributing to the problem whilst they are paying the price.

Thief

If you sit at a pavement café you are likely to find yourself people-watching. If you are sitting on a boat on the edge of a lake, you will more likely find yourself birdwatching. My eyes had been following a tern as it patrolled its territory, occasionally swooping low as if it had seen something in the water but then it would lift off at the last moment. My attention was beginning to wander when it suddenly dived, barely grazing the surface, and lifted off with a small fish in its beak. Within a few seconds another tern appeared, then another, both mobbing the first bird. It wheeled and dived but they mirrored its movements, an aerial dance with one bird determined to hold on to its food and the others focused on stealing it. They disappeared behind the treeline, leaving me to wonder how the story ended.

Is it a normal pattern of behaviour for birds and animals to steal from each other? I thought of two cats of mine from years ago, one an effective mouser, the other less so. I would often see the less-skilled hunter take a newly caught mouse from the jaws of the other. And then there were my chickens, back in the days when we had our smallholding. The supply of eggs tended to fluctuate depending on who got to them first, me or the magpies. Eggs are prized bounty for numerous creatures, foxes, pine martens, stoats, weasels and rats, as well as crows, ravens and jays. I hadn't realised that hedgehogs, one of those animals that we usually regard with fondness, are not above a spot of breaking and entering with thievery on their mind. Apparently they will drive the birds off their nest, steal the egg, bite a hole and then lick the contents as they drip out. Not so sweet after all.

There is an official name to describe the action of one animal stealing from another, *kleptoparasites*, and it seems commonplace across many species. As the cuckoo is infamous for laying its egg in another bird's nest, effectively stealing a place by subterfuge, so the cuckoo bee does much the same thing. As its larvae hatch they eat the larvae of the host bee, giving a whole new meaning to the idea of bed and breakfast.

Magpies have a reputation for stealing jewellery and trinkets, as well as eggs, but official studies have not found this to be the case. The satin bowerbird from Australia has a penchant for blue objects as the males use feathers from other birds, shells, flowers, plastic straws or bottle caps to decorate their nests and attract females.

There aren't many creatures bold enough to steal from humans but one of the most well known is the seagull. Nicknamed the 'pirates of the seashore', they can't dive and catch fish for themselves so they will steal it from other gulls and birds, from otters and from humans. In the latter case if it comes with a portion of chips or a sandwich, so much the better.

We humans are probably the biggest kleptoparasites of all. We take honey from bees, eggs from chickens, milk from cows. We kill elephants for their tusks, rhinos for their horns, and tigers for their skins. It's common practice for us to steal from each other. Sometimes, standing back from my own humanity and looking at my species with objective eyes is a sobering exercise.

July

Strawberries and cream and a soft summer breeze

The elusive kingfisher

A kingfisher flits along the riverbank, a flash of midnight blue. It whistles a cheeky *now you see me, now you don't* refrain as it disappears yet again into the undergrowth. Kingfishers are elusive birds and so often we only spot them as they fly away. Being on the water means that we are well placed to see the nests of birds, many in full view, but I have never seen a kingfisher's nest and I wondered where they hide themselves away. The answer was as intriguing as the bird itself.

They build a tunnel in a bank, at least a metre long, sloping upwards so it won't easily flood. If the chosen site is by the water the male bird will pick a position high enough to avoid flooding, but sometimes they are far from the water, perhaps in a ditch or a sandpit where the soil might be looser. They don't seem to be natural excavators, and indeed carving out a nest this way is a huge job for such a small bird. It begins with the male flying at the bank head first and using his bill to loosen the surface layer. Once he has made a small ledge, work can begin in earnest. It can take a couple of weeks to construct the nest site and so the pair will take turns, the bird who is digging always watched over by its mate. The tunnel is narrow and so they have to shuffle backwards to get out, kicking away any loose soil with their feet.

At the end of the tunnel they make a larger chamber, big enough for up to seven eggs and angled so that there is no danger of them rolling out. Kingfishers cough up pellets of indigestible material in much the same way that owls do, and in the spirit of waste not, want not these pellets, made of fish bones and scales, are broken up and used as additional insulation for the nest. When a kingfisher can exit a nest site head first it is a sign that the nesting chamber is nearly finished.

If food has been plentiful the chicks will be ready to leave the nest after approximately 20 days, a bit longer if food has been scarce. Each chick consumes a surprising number of fish a day, which means the parents have to work hard, and also means that the nest gets increasingly smelly as a pile of rotting fish bits and bones builds up.

Once the chicks have fledged they are fed for a few days more and then driven from the nest so that the adult birds can lay eggs for their next brood. Given the state of the nesting chamber at this point they may well begin a new tunnel afresh, although some old tunnels are cleared out and used again. The pair will remain together for this breeding season, but will find a new mate for the following year.

Nature can be incredibly efficient at times, and then it all falls apart and to human eyes it seems tragic. The fledglings are sometimes ill-equipped to survive alone. Some will become waterlogged and drown. Others have not mastered the art of fishing effectively and will starve. Estimates vary on how many survive, ranging from a quarter to half of them dying within a few weeks. Because the adult birds produce a reasonable number of chicks in each batch and have two, perhaps three, broods a season the species survives but it seems that it could tip either way so easily. I would have expected to see more kingfishers in these quiet waterways and wonder if their numbers are declining.

The next time I saw a kingfisher I looked at it with different eyes. I had great respect and admiration for how hard they work to build their tunnel and feed their chicks, tinged with a sadness for how precarious life is. Many of us in the west have managed to protect ourselves from such a knife-edge existence in so many ways, but I suspect the truth is that our lives are also precarious. It's just as well none of us, human or animal or bird, know what the future holds.

Watching me, watching you

I had gone out for a walk, making the most of a rare moment when the rain had temporarily eased, trying to regain a sense of equilibrium rather than irritation at the unseasonably wet summer weather. Walking down a grassy track that opened out onto a field I happened to look up just as a hare hopped out of the bushes, perfectly framed by the trees that arched over from either side of the path.

I looked at the hare and it looked at me, one of those rare, incredibly precious moments when you get a sense of real connection. Neither of us moved. I was close enough to see how big its eyes were, glassy and protuberant. And those wonderful ears, somehow too big for the rest of the body, both comical and endearing.

The only thing I know about hares is that they go a little

mad in March. I've always assumed that when hares are seen boxing it is two males, seeking to impress or claim a female, and at times this might be so, but it is just as likely to be a female who has tired of the overly-persistent attentions of a male and has decided it's time to put him in his place.

Eventually my hare must have decided I was nothing to worry about and gave up the staring match. It began to eat, crouching low, half-hidden in the grass, flattening its ears along its back. Their eyesight is triggered by movement and if you stay still long enough there is a chance that they will come close, unaware that you are there. Wildlife photographer Rich Steel recounts in his blog an unexpected meeting with a hare that walked right up to him while he was sitting in the hedge line and actually started licking his boot, perhaps attracted by the residue of salt from an earlier walk along the beach. He suggests that if you really want to get close it is best to crawl flat on your belly as they associate an upright human with danger.

I decided that today was not a day for crawling about in the grass and instead wondered what my hare actually saw when he, or she, looked at me. Indeed what does any animal or bird see when they look at a human being? They certainly don't perceive us in the same way that we view ourselves, some seeing in a limited sense whilst others command a more sophisticated view of the world. Bees have no red receptors and so what seems like a vibrant red to us will probably be some combination of blue-green, blue or violet to them. Snakes can sense infra-red and thermal images. Birds of prey can focus over long distances, to the point where we might see just a field but they can see a mouse hidden in the grass.

As for hares, they are flight animals, their eyes placed high to the side of their head, giving them almost 360 degrees of vision, a vital tool in detecting and evading predators. However they have a small blind spot, directly in front of their face, and this explains why they don't always see stationary objects that are directly in front of them. Humans can detect red, blue and green light but hares see only in blue and green and whilst they can see more clearly than us in the low light of dusk and dawn, their resolution is not so good in bright light, giving their world a grainy feel to it.

I had been standing quite still, hare-watching, for long enough. I backed away, slowly, but within a second the hare's head came up, its head swivelled in my direction and it shot off, jumping cleanly over the ditch and out across the field. I watched it run, envying its grace and wishing, just for a second, that I could experience the elation of being able to fly over the ground so effortlessly. Instead, I turned back, feeling heavy and slow, a lumbering human being. The hare can reach speeds of 40 mph and I can't even match that on my bike.

As I left the little copse of trees behind me the evening sun suddenly broke free from behind a bank of clouds, bathing the clearing in that wonderfully rich light that only comes at the end of the day. All my niggling feelings about the weather disappeared, wiped clean by the beauty of the moment and by the good fortune to have had a quiet encounter with a hare.

Water lily

A tiny duckling hopped onto a lily pad. It was a young one, still fluffy, but even at this age it was developing an independent nature. Some ducklings never stray far from their mother, appearing to have an invisible tether that keeps them close, but occasionally one of the brood is born with rebel genes. This one pecked away at the surface of the pad with enthusiasm, mirroring the actions of its mother, although it seemed to me that it wasn't entirely sure what the point of the exercise was at this stage.

It was so engrossed in exploring what the lily pad had to offer that it hadn't noticed that its mother had moved on and was now some distance away. Suddenly going it alone didn't seem such a good idea. It shot across the lily pad stepping stones, and threw itself into the water, tiny feet paddling away with all its strength, panic written in every line until it caught her up. Then it staggered up onto another lily pad and plonked itself down. Time to take a breather.

I suspect our little duckling views the green lily pads as the primary attraction of this plant, but I love the flowers. I am not alone in being drawn to them. Monet was so enchanted by them that he produced over 250 paintings. The flowers only last for around four days before sinking beneath the water, decomposing and nourishing future generations. We have seen pink and white blooms on these waterways, but they come in a huge variety of colours and grow all around the world. They seem to have some special quality to them, a purity and perfection that can't be sullied. I often watch in fascination as we cruise past them, the drag from our wash pulling the flower right under the water. Once we have passed it resurfaces, still perfect, still beautiful, despite the fact that the water here is the colour of tea due to the peaty nature of the surrounding landscape. Buddhists believe the flower represents enlightenment, a pristine bloom emerging from muddy waters, and also resurrection due to the fact that the flowers close up at night and open again every morning, a symbol of a new beginning.

Apparently the lily is July's birth flower. In much the same way as we are all born under a star sign, so there are also two flowers assigned to each month, one primary and one secondary to accommodate the fact that not all cultures agree on the choice of flower. These flowers have qualities that may, or may not depending on whether you believe in such things, be passed on to people born in that month. Until this point I hadn't been aware that such a thing as a birth flower existed and had a passing fancy to see which flowers had been chosen.

January – carnation and snowdrop
February – violet and iris or primrose
March – daffodil and jonquil (type of daffodil)
April – daisy and sweet pea
May – lily of the valley and hawthorn
June – rose and honeysuckle
July – delphinium and water lily
August – gladiolus and poppy

September – aster and morning glory

October – marigold and cosmos

November – chrysanthemum

December – holly and narcissus

It has been suggested that the idea of having a particular flower, or flowers, for each month of the year originated from Roman times, which is when birthdays first began. Over the centuries it has evolved into a belief that each flower has a particular symbolism and can hold special meaning for people born in that month. For example, people born in the month of the poppy could be honest and faithful with great integrity whilst the lily of the valley shares sweetness and purity. The honeysuckle bestows happiness and positive energy and the water lily represents purity and innocence. I was born in September and my flowers are asters and morning glory. Purple asters are considered a royal colour and bestow wisdom. White asters represent innocence, red ones devotion and passion, and pink ones bring love and kindness. Each colour of the morning glory also has different properties, ranging from power to grace, wealth, strength, purity and innocence. I fear quite a few of these properties seem to have passed me by, particularly the one about wealth, but hopefully someone, somewhere has reaped the benefits.

If I could choose my own two flowers, which would they be? I think poppies and water lilies would come top of the list. Or perhaps roses and daffodils. Or perhaps it's impossible to choose when they are all so beautiful.

Cruel to be kind

The Netherlands is a perfect habitat for white storks, and we have learnt to keep an eye out for their nests, usually perched on posts six to eight metres above the ground. These nests are impressive structures, and their weight and size will vary depending on their location. If they can find a deserted house or barn, or a chimney where they won't be disturbed, the nests can grow as wide as two metres, a staggering two to three metres in height and weigh up to a tonne. It takes time to build such a structure and so they prefer to expand and repair a nest from the previous breeding season. They add sticks, hay, straw and manure and over the years these successive layers decompose and become soil, which explains why it is so heavy. They are opportunistic builders, not averse to including plastic bags, socks, gloves and hats – even boxer shorts have been recycled and put to good use. Some nests have been used for over 50 years.

These birds have coexisted alongside humans for many years, although you need to be something of a dedicated stork lover to give your chimney up to a bird standing a metre high and with a wingspan of over two metres. In the Netherlands, Germany and eastern Europe it was believed that a stork nest on your roof brought good luck and that they were a symbol of good parenting and strong family bonds. Hans Christian Andersen wrote a fable where storks plucked a dreaming baby from a pond or lake and delivered it to deserving families. However families with children who misbehaved would receive a dead baby as a warning. Not such a happy ending.

There is a darker side to stork family life. It is not common practice but storks have been known to kill their babies. It happens when food is in short supply and there isn't enough to go round. The adult will choose the smallest and weakest baby and simply drop them from the nest. At such a height the outcome is both predictable and inevitable.

There are 20 species of stork but parental infanticide has only been recorded in two species, the white stork and the black stork. The young chicks of these two specific species are not competitive, an unusual trait as most chicks will fight and jostle for food. It's a natural, survival-of-the-fittest strategy that weeds out the weakest, who will often die for lack of food as a result. Without this built-in culling process, the burden falls to the adult.

Their eggs don't all hatch at the same time, and sometimes the latest egg to hatch can be substantially behind the older chicks. The one who comes last is at the greatest risk of being despatched. Rather than being ejected from the nest a newly-born chick might be shaken until it dies and then eaten, presumably on the instinctive reaction that if food is in short supply, nothing should be wasted.

Nature, for the most part, doesn't have the luxury of being compassionate or sentimental. I never personally saw evidence of young chicks being killed in this way, although it has been well documented and filmed and was confirmed when we visited a stork breeding station that was fortuitously on our route. The birds don't do it with any malicious intent or to be deliberately cruel, but simply to protect the strongest of the brood and give them the best chance in life. To our human eyes of course, it is shocking, heart-breaking, but there is a danger in looking at nature through rose-tinted spectacles. It just doesn't work that way.

AUGUST

Summer whispers a sad farewell and autumn rises to take her place

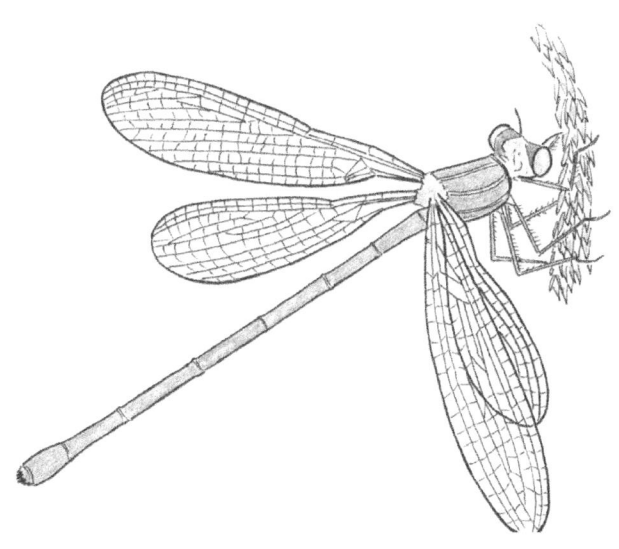

Wondrous willow

It was a Sunday and the waterway we were on was closed for the day or, to be more accurate, the bridge-keepers weren't there to lift bridges and that effectively stops all movement. Boating tends to be a seven-days-a-week activity, and the weekends are often the busiest, but we were on the eastern border of the Netherlands, a place that fewer people travelled to, and on a little-used waterway.

We had moored up against the bank, just in front of one of these bridges, and were enjoying a day of going nowhere. We are hopeless at going slowly, always moving on, and on the rare occasions when we have no option but to remain still for the day, it feels like a proper holiday rather than a way of life.

I watched a pair of linnets darting in and out of a willow tree, so close that I could almost touch them from where I was sitting on the deck. I had to resort to my bird book to identify this particular bird and was quite disappointed that it was described as a common linnet. They didn't seem at all common to me with their striking red breast and forehead. I found them quite beautiful and so for a while they took all my attention but eventually I started to look more closely at the tree itself. There is something inherently appealing about a willow tree but I wondered if it was purely its beauty that made this tree worthy of note. It turned out that there was much more to the willow tree than I had realised.

Historically we have a special relationship with this species, one that has been woven into the fabric of our lives for hundreds of years, a link so strong that at times it ceased to be just a tree and became a friend and a partner. It has long been associated with healing. Our ancestors used to chew the bark, releasing a compound that provided pain relief for colds, fevers, headaches and toothaches. They also boiled the bark in water and then drank the liquid to relieve diarrhoea and reduce inflammation from arthritis. They gargled with it for sore throats, used it to clean wounds and to stop bleeding.

All these processes released a compound in the bark called salicin, one that is found in all the Salix species. In 1859 Professor Hermann Kolbe at Marburg University in Germany was the first scientist to identify the chemical structure of salicylic acid but it was another scientist at Bayer & Co who pulled the threads together and successfully produced a synthetic version of the natural remedy. It was registered on February 1st 1899, the first time a drug had been produced synthetically, and was credited with instigating the birth of the pharmaceuticals industry. It is a drug we are all familiar with and it goes by the name of Aspirin.

In the past we have also relied on the willow for shelter and transport. It was used as a framework for homes and boats. The Dutch made their clogs from it, the Celts made spokes for chariot wheels, gypsies made clothes pegs and others made a dye from the bark for tanning leather. In Scotland they made anchor rope, taking advantage of the fibrous and pliable nature of the bark, and used strips of bark to tie down the thatch on roofs. Willow stems were ideal for baskets, coffins, lobster pots and beehives.

We have seen it ourselves this summer, as the Dutch use it as an edging to protect the banks of the rivers and canals from the erosion caused by the wash from passing boats. It's not just practical either. It can be used in art and sculpture, often using live cuttings that are woven in situ. Above all, willow is a sustainable resource as its regrowth is vigorous.

Reflecting on the myriad ways that we had used the willow over all those years, I was struck by how I mostly referred to them in the past tense. Basket making is still carried out, often as a hobby and not on the scale that it would have been years ago, but for the most part we have found other ways to do things. An inevitable consequence of this shift is that the tree-lore, built up and refined over the years, passed from one generation to another, slowly disappears, made redundant in a world where we manufacture almost everything we need, much of it from plastic or concrete, and give scant regard to the long-term sustainability of the process.

For a moment I allowed myself to dwell on an apocalyptic scenario where all the modern trappings of life disappeared. Leaving aside the specific nature of the disaster, although there are no shortage of possible candidates, how would I fare in a world where I could no longer count on Google or YouTube for answers and where no older family members had any basic survival skills to pass on?

How would I feel about stripping off some willow bark and

chewing it when I had chronic toothache? If I wanted to boil it up and make a liquid painkiller how much bark should I use, how long should I boil it for and what would happen if I made it too strong? Would my attempt at a willow shelter hold up in a storm? Would my coracle sink or float? My world would become full of questions without answers, an incomprehensible situation compared to the world I live in now, with all knowledge just a click away.

In front of me the willow tree sighed with pleasure as a warm wind ran its fingers through the branches. The future was not something that it bothered about and I would do well to emulate such a pragmatic outlook. Even so, it wouldn't do any harm to keep a lookout for a book on old herbal remedies...

Dancing jewel

'Where do dragonflies get their name from?' I mused quietly to myself as I watched them dancing their way through the reeds and over the water lilies.

'Because they're so big,' myself promptly replied.

'But they're not all big. Those big blue ones are huge, but see those red ones? So dainty.'

It soon became apparent that I was woefully ignorant when it came down to dragonflies. To begin with, I had been lumping dragonflies and damselflies together, when in fact they are different. They both belong to the insect order of Odonata, meaning 'toothed jaw' but they are in two different suborders. Damselflies, of the suborder Zygoptera, meaning 'equal-winged', have a more delicate appearance, long and thin, whilst dragonflies, who are of the suborder Anisoptera, meaning 'unequal-winged', are short and stocky.

I knew that Latin names and suborders of species would never stick in my mind and also suspected that my skills of observation would not be sufficient to be able to tell whether the hindwings were shorter than the forewings as these beautiful creatures flew around me at great speed. However I did find another good way for the beginner naturist to tell them apart. Dragonflies rest with their wings out from their bodies, often at right angles, whereas damselflies fold them back in along their stomachs. Once I was aware of this simple distinction, I noticed it all the time and felt a thrill of pleasure at having learnt something I could retain and use.

As to how they got their name, there are a number of possible explanations. The Romanians referred to dragonflies as the devil's fly. Their word for devil is 'drac' but they use that same word for dragon and so the theory is that somewhere along the line the two were mixed up and translated into dragonfly. This seems a tenuous link but the history of how things got their names often seems questionable.

Another explanation is based on the physical properties of the dragonfly and I found this to be more probable. They have fantastic flight abilities, able to twist and turn at speed in every direction: up and down, side to side, forwards and even flying backwards. You only have to spend a few moments watching them to see how finely controlled their movements are. They are also frighteningly efficient hunters if you are unlucky enough to be on their list of preferred foods. Smaller insects are taken straight into the mouth, but they catch larger ones with their feet, tear off their wings so that their prey can't escape, making use of those toothed jaws that give them their name, and then swallow the rest of the insect whole. Depending on the particular species of dragonfly they may consume their dinner on the wing or retire to a nearby leaf or twig. Strangely, they have six legs but can't walk. Their eyesight is impressive, compound eyes made up of 30,000 individual lenses, allowing them to locate their prey with great precision. This combination of flight skills, those serrated teeth and a voracious appetite are thought to be another reason why they are called dragonflies and one that certainly makes more sense to me.

As befits any creature with the word dragon as part of its name there are myths and legends aplenty with which to while away an afternoon. One of their many common names is the Devil's Darning Needles and the story warns of falling asleep by a stream on a sunny day, particularly if you are a naughty child or have the bad habit of lying to people. The damselfly, so ethereal, so delicate, has a darker side and will sew your eyes together while you slumber. In Norway the common name for the species is Eyepoker; in Portugal they refer to them as Eye Snatchers. According to Swedish legend trolls used dragonflies as spindles when weaving their clothes, hence their common name of Troll's Spindles.

There are around 7,000 species of true dragonflies and they all have the necessary Latin names, one example being *Agriocnemis pinheyi*. I can't even pronounce this and, as I don't understand Latin, it gives me no clue as to what this dragonfly looks like. To be fair, neither does its common name, Pinhey's Wisp, but it sounds so much more appealing, conjuring up an image of sunlight through gossamer wings, as insubstantial as a wisp of mist rising over the river.

I've compiled a short list of some of my favourite common names of dragonflies from all around the world below. Often they describe the vibrant colours that are so typical of these astonishing insects, or the way that they move, darting and skimming, or they might even draw a comparison to their hunting skills with words like hawk and widow. I'll leave you to browse the list below and let your imagination conjure up an image to suit the name.

Vagrant Darter
Broad-bodied Chaser
Downy Emerald
Blue-eyed Darner
Azure Hawker
Widow Skimmer
Great Pond-hawk
Dancing Jewel
Yellow-faced Sprite
Orange Emperor
Jaunty Dropwing

One for sorrow

A single magpie perched on a rooftop and stared at me with a bright and beady eye. I'd left the boat for a walk through the back streets of the town where we had moored up for the night, needing to stretch my legs. Anxiously, and hardly aware that I was doing it, I looked around to see if this magpie had a mate. A second bird flew up to join it and I let out a sigh of relief. I am not a remotely superstitious person and yet, without fail, I will count magpies and recite the rhyme to myself.

One for sorrow, two for joy
Three for a girl, four for a boy
Five for silver, six for gold
Seven for a secret, never to be told

In later years more verses were added on.

Eight for a wish, nine for a kiss
Ten for a bird you must not miss
Eleven for health, twelve for wealth
Thirteen beware, it's the devil himself

This ancient rhyme originates in British folklore, being first recorded in 1780. The oldest version had a different theme and didn't rhyme.

One for sorrow, two for joy
Three for a funeral, four for a birth
Five for heaven, six for hell
Seven for the devil, his own self

The magpies were still sitting on top of the roof and the sun caught their tail feathers. In my mind they are a black and white bird, clearly defined and handsome with it, but if you look closely at their wings and their long tail in the right light you can see that they have an iridescent sheen of blue and purple, similar to a peacock or a male mallard. They are striking birds, highly intelligent, and I wondered why the superstition and legend that surrounds them portrays them in such a bad light.

As is the way with all folklore, the devil and witchcraft are never far away, so it came as no surprise to learn that early Christians believed that magpies carried a drop of the devil's blood under their tongue, making them a vessel of evil spirits. One tale holds that the magpie was either the only bird not allowed in Noah's Ark or that it was the only bird that refused to go into it and that it sat on the top instead and swore while the world drowned. I'd love to know what it was saying.

They are maligned for the way they will raid the nests of other birds to provide food for their own chicks but something is always eating something else in the natural world, and they only do this in the breeding season, feeding on wild berries and seeds, worms and molluscs for the rest of the year.

They are very loyal birds and mate for life which might

explain the first verse of the rhyme and puts an entirely different perspective on it. A lone bird without its mate will be a sad one whereas a pair are happy. The sorrow relates to how the bird feels, not to a state of mind that it will inflict upon the human who happens to look at it at the wrong time.

I feel pleased with this new insight, but a little voice inside my head whispers that I should still look for two birds, not the one, just to be on the safe side. Some habits are hard to break.

Suppose we weren't here

One of the personal lessons I have learned whilst writing this book is that I know very little about most things. However, this is one topic where I feel I might reasonably claim to know what I am talking about.

Late summer every year we return to our cabin home near the Pyrenees after four to six months away on our boat. Each spring we leave the flower borders free of weeds, the grass immediately around the cabin neat, and the rest of the field orderly after its annual cut, after which we leave it to grow wild. By the time we come back, however, nature has completely taken over, and done so with great vigour and enthusiasm.

The first clue as to how much hard work we are facing to restore order comes at the front gate. A metal grating gives us access over a small stream which runs down the side of our land. The stream bed is usually almost dry by this time of the year, but it provides a fertile base for ash seedlings to take root and then push their way through the open grating. We have to pick our way over a mini-forest, interspersed with tendrils of bramble that snag on my legs as if to say I am not welcome here. I can imagine the look of weary resignation from our post lady as she has seen this obstacle course grow higher each month, making it ever more challenging to reach our mailbox.

Le Shack is situated in the corner of approximately two acres of field, all now waist-high with grass, wildflowers, and many more oak and ash saplings, all of which is good, but also bramble, bracken and gorse which is not quite so good. The track that runs across the field, one that we keep mown as our second point of access, has disappeared as if it had never been. The wisteria, so elegant and refined when we left, has grown into a monster after a summer of rampant growth and wrapped itself in a death embrace around the wing mirrors and roof of our old camper van, showing no sign of being willing to let go. A little further up the hill is the caravan, which I use as my writing room, but this track also is completely overgrown and the brambles are climbing up the door.

Further down the hill, below the cabin, the composting bins have become a mound-shaped support for wild honeysuckle. The small flower beds around the cabin are full of weeds, the pond is choked with algae, and the spiders have claimed ownership of our outside composting loo and adjoining summer kitchen, which sounds grander than it is, being no more than a sink and drainer.

Armed with a broom I begin the fight to re-establish our right to go to the loo without fear of a spider descending from the rafters above or of walking into a web sneakily positioned at head height. The size of some of the webs, not to mention their inhabitants, is worthy of respect but I can feel my face screwing up in distaste at the collection of dead bodies held fast in those silky threads: a wing of a butterfly, what might have been a cricket in another life and sundry small body parts. Looking more closely I realise that there are two very large spiders that also look past their best. As I gently poke the web with a stick, a smaller spider scuttles across in the hope of lunch and, realising that it was a false alarm, disappears inside what is left of one of its larger brethren.

It's not all bad news. This year we have returned a few weeks earlier than usual and the wildflowers are still out en masse, jostling for space and weaving a tapestry of lilac and cream, while the butterflies delicately pick and choose the best specimens. I spotted a praying mantis perched on the weeds in the flower bed and an alarmingly large white beetle that I was unable to identify had taken up temporary residence in one of the flower pots. Wildlife tracks wove through the tall grasses and we found fox droppings two paces from our front door. They never come that close when we are in residence and the thought crossed my mind as to who the intruder is here. We bought this property and feel that we own it, but the wildlife was here long before we were and has no awareness of money and what it can buy you.

Each year we return to this scenario and each time I find myself awestruck at the irrepressible force of the natural world. It is simply unstoppable. We humans do our best to tame it, endlessly toiling in our gardens, cutting, clipping, weeding and trimming, week in, week out, as obsessed with keeping everything tidy as nature is determined to be wildly unruly. Out in the wider world we concrete over it so that we can build our cities, homes and factories or spray it with pesticides to protect our crops.

How would it feel if the human race suddenly disappeared from the Earth? As you can see I experience the answer to that question every time we return home after a long summer away, but what I see is the effect on one small patch of land over just a few months. The consequences would be much harder to imagine and understand on a global scale.

Perhaps one of the first things we would notice would be how much quieter it was. No planes, trains, lorries, cars or tractors. No lawnmowers and chain saws, no forklift trucks and air-conditioning units humming away night and day. No human voices. We had some experience of this during the first pandemic. We returned to *Olivia Rose* in France four days before the first lockdown in 2020. Suddenly there were no cars on the road, no children in the school playground. That abrupt tumble into a silent world was surreal and I can still recall how it shocked me.

If we weren't here it's likely that the wind and the rain would slowly wash away the smog, dust and pollution that we used to produce every day. Skies would be more vividly blue and the air would become cleaner. With no-one to maintain our national grid, the pumping stations would fall silent, flooding the underground transport systems. With no-one in charge of oil refineries and nuclear plants there would be sporadic fires and explosions. In our homes there would be no heating, no lights, and the water pipes would burst after the first frost. Our gardens and parks would very quickly look just like our own wilderness does now, whilst tree roots would push up through pavements and cities would become forests.

For the natural world this sudden lack of human activity would set off a chain reaction of a different nature. There are many different possible scenarios but one of them imagines that without the steady release of pesticides, chemicals and other pollutants, insect life would proliferate, in turn leading to greater pollination of plants. Animals, birds and insects would flourish as habitats naturally restored themselves, the larger predators would slowly return and the food chain might just rebalance itself. Human noise would be replaced by a cacophony of buzzing and chirping and the creatures who had felt the need to hide in the woods and wild places in order to survive whilst humans dominated the planet would gradually build up the confidence to walk openly once more.

It provides some small solace to think that the planet could restore balance and carry on without us, even though it would take thousands of years for the types of changes described above to take place and there are many other factors that could derail the process. And the consequences of climate change, the legacy we leave behind us, are set on a course that won't stop just because we are no longer here.

Our time living in this very special patch of wilderness has taught us that there are some battles you can't win. Each year the part of the field that we call ours gets a little smaller and the part belonging to the wildlife gets bigger. We do our best to hold back the invasive species that would be detrimental to the diversity we so enjoy but, mostly, we leave nature to glory in her excess.

There is one area where we take no prisoners, however, and that is our composting loo. There are some lines that cannot be crossed and I know that tomorrow I shall be back out with my broom again after the spiders have had a busy night spinning away. It might take me a few weeks but this is one battle I know I can win and there is no shame in small victories.

SEPTEMBER

The harvest is in and the season is turning

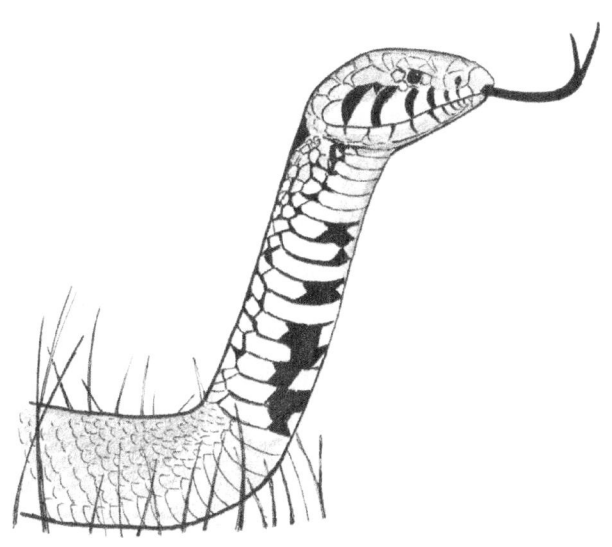

Reflecting on reflections

Reflections always take me by surprise. I can sit by the pond at Le Shack, intently gazing at the water, waiting for a newt to float to the surface or, if I am lucky, perhaps I might catch the elusive flash of a salamander, but then I will suddenly realise that the clouds are perfectly reflected in the water. And then I'll notice that I can see a mirror image of the hazel bushes, of an old tree stump and a couple of rocks. If I lean forward I am looking at a mirror image of myself.

Another day at another time, as the sun slips below the horizon and I stand again by the pond, mesmerised by a purple and scarlet sky streaked with tangerine, it is only as I turn away that my eye falls lower and sees that same sunset recreated on the surface of the water.

I could tell you that reflections are produced as rays of sunlight bounce off the trees onto the pond surface, and then into our eyes. And the image of the reflection is upside down because the light hits the water at a certain angle. If you wanted to know more we could talk about the density of the water compared to the density of the air and concepts such as vertical inversion but I think we'll leave it there and simply enjoy the reflections for what they are. As Mark Twain so wisely said, 'We have not the reverent feeling for the rainbow that the savage has, because we know how it is made. We have lost as much as we have gained by prying into that matter.'

I return to my study of the reflections on the water, noting how they flicker and disappear as a light breeze ruffles the surface, and carefully refrain from asking myself why that should be. It's good to ask questions, but we don't always need an answer.

Celestial beast

I love the long summer nights but the downside is that there are months where I go to bed before it is truly dark and don't get to see the stars. The autumn equinox will soon be upon us, the nights are drawing in and it feels as if I am welcoming back old friends. The first constellation that I look for is the Plough. Some stars rise and set in much the same way as the sun, but the Plough stays up all night. It looks down on me 365 days of the year, albeit in varying orientations, and bestows a feeling of permanence and stability.

It has such a distinctive shape, so easy to pinpoint, each of its seven individual stars shining so clearly. In Western astronomy stars are usually named in Arabic and the stars that make up the Plough have a pleasingly exotic ring to them: Alcor, Mizar, Alioth, Megrez, Phecda, Merak and Dubhe.

The Plough is also referred to as the Great Bear, or Ursa Major, and this has always puzzled me. Why call it that when it doesn't look like a bear?

The answer lies in the bigger picture. The Plough is not a constellation in its own right but is one segment of Ursa Major.

This much larger constellation does indeed look like a bear and the Plough can either represent its hindquarters and tail or the back of its head and neck, running down into the back. It all becomes clear once you see the shape of the entire constellation.

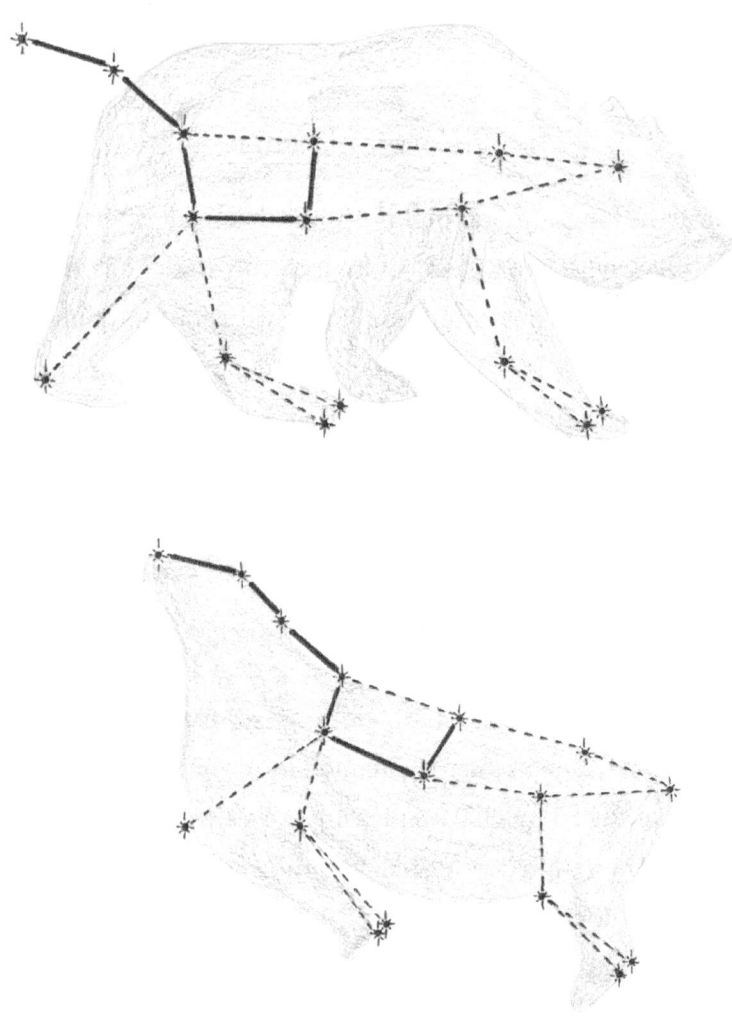

I gaze at the stars just for the pleasure of it but historically mankind has relied on the position of the Plough to guide them in the way they live. In medieval Britain farmers would decide when to sow and plough their fields using the position of the Plough for reassurance that their timing was right. Similarly Native American tribes used the orientation of the Big Dipper (their name for the same collection of stars as it resembled a ladle or a water dipper) as a tool for decisions on which hunting grounds to visit, or which foods to plant. These ancient cultures looked for ways to understand and explain their world, just as we still do, but where we now rely heavily on technology, they looked to the heavens. They also used stories as a way to share that understanding and pass it on to future generations. One such tale describes a group of hunters chasing the bear through the sky. One of their arrows wounded it, although not fatally, and as the injured creature swooped low to the horizon his blood fell and stained the leaves on the trees. And that is why we have autumn.

Snake in the grass

'I've just seen a snake,' said Michael. 'In fact, I almost stepped on it.'

'Where was it? Did it do anything?' I asked eagerly.

'It was on the track. I had no idea it was there until it reared up and hissed at me. Thankfully it slithered off into the grass and disappeared after that.' He sounded a little rattled by the experience.

'I wish I had seen it. How big was it?'

'Too big.' He gave an involuntary shiver. 'I don't like snakes.'

Most of us don't like snakes, although it's quite difficult to pinpoint why our sense of aversion is so strong. There is something so alien, so 'other' about them that we feel threatened and yet, for the most part, they are shy creatures, far more likely to get out of our way as fast as they can rather than confront us. It is usually only when they feel threatened or cornered that they strike.

When we have strong feelings about a creature, be they negative or positive, they are often based in stories and myths that are part of our culture. For example, most of us know the story of Adam and Eve, with the snake convincing Eve to eat the forbidden apple. In Chinese mythology a snake with a woman's head amused herself by making the first humans out of clay. One by one, she modelled them and watched them come to life. Her first humans became high class, the latter models lower class, bringing a new insight into the phrase 'an accident of birth'.

Looking back over the centuries snakes have been all things to all people. They are associated with healing, with wisdom and good luck. In ancient Greek mythology Asclepius would send his snake familiars out in the night to visit the sick who had come to sleep in his shrine. The snakes slithered over the bodies and licked them back to health. You would hope no-one woke up during the process – the stuff of nightmares indeed.

On the other hand, think of as many unpleasant characteristics as you can and they might well refer to a snake, words like evil, cunning, devious, deceitful, untrustworthy and malevolent.

Their physical attributes reinforce these negative impressions. They have a sinister air about them, with glassy, watchful eyes that don't blink and that forked tongue, flicking in and out. In reality their tongue is how they smell and surely there can be nothing menacing about that. A special organ in the roof of their mouth, known as Jacobson's organ, allows them to read and recognise the scent molecules in the air and the forked nature of their tongue allows them to tell which direction the smell is coming from. The next time I see a snake with its head lifted, flicking its tongue, I shall understand why it is doing it and I suspect it won't bother me in the way it has previously.

The snake that Michael stumbled across was most likely a grass snake, known as *couleuvre* in French, although vipers are also commonly found here in the south west corner of the country. The female grass snake grows up to two metres long whilst the males are smaller, on average about 60cm. Like all snakes they cannot create their own body heat and rely on the sun to warm them up and so it's possible it was simply sunning itself when Michael happened upon it. They hear through internal ear bones rather than external ones and are also aware of vibrations through the ground. If Michael had stomped a little harder as he walked down the track the snake would have had more time to get out of the way.

Snakes provides an interesting example of how the model of the food chain works so efficiently for ensuring a balanced ecosystem. Our grass snake is not a venomous species, and whilst it does have teeth they are used only for gripping. It relies on stealth and ambush, grabbing and swallowing its prey whole, whether it be a lizard or frog, a small mammal or bird. There is every chance the unfortunate creature will still be alive as it is swallowed. The snake, in turn, is preyed upon by other creatures, all of which reside in the woods around us: badgers, owls, magpies, foxes, martens and wild boar. What goes around comes around and so the merry-go-round keeps turning.

Michael was seeing a common defence mechanism when the grass snake reared up and hissed at him. He was lucky that he didn't experience the other weapon in its arsenal, which is to emit a harmless but foul-smelling and long- lasting odour from its anal glands. As a final resort, if cornered they will 'play dead', lying on their backs with their head twisted, mouth wide and tongue lolling in a macabre death rictus. It seems a wonderfully theatrical response and even has an official name, thanatosis behaviour, but it doesn't always pay off, in which case they have rendered themselves vulnerable to an unhappy final scene.

Armed with this new knowledge I feel differently about snakes and am even sadder that I didn't get to see the one Michael almost trod on. I think they have had a bad press that they largely don't deserve. I might feel differently if I lived in Australia and had to contend with some much more dangerous snakes but I am more than happy to share our personal paradise with the species that live in this corner of France. As with all creatures, it is best to abide by the rules of giving them space and trying to avoid confrontational situations where possible.

Blind as a bat

Nocturnal animals live in a different world to those of us who function best in the hours of daylight. The creatures of the night have adapted to survive in this unique environment, and few are more skilled at navigating and hunting in the dark than the bat.

As a child I can remember being subjected to the old wives' tale of how bats will fly into your hair and get so entangled that they have to be cut out with a pair of scissors, a convenient story used by parents to keep their children from staying out too late at night. In some ways it worked, as for years the thought of a bat flying around my head evoked a sense of panic. Standing in the dark outside our cabin, many years later, I no longer have that fear. The bats fly around me as they do every night, a flicker of movement out of the corner of my eye, so fast, so controlled, so focused, so aware. They are consummate fliers and there is no chance whatsoever of them accidentally bumping into me and my hair.

I can appreciate their aerobatics but I don't understand how they do it. How is it possible to flip and twist at such speed in the pitch black of night without ever making an error? Despite the old saying of being 'blind as a bat' they have good eyesight, even at night, but they also use their ears to build up a highly detailed evaluation of their environment and what is in it.

In our visual system of sight we rely on light reflected from objects around us. In contrast, bats can also 'see' through sound being reflected from objects, analysing the echoes that bounce back as the sound comes into contact with a tree or a building. This technique is known as 'echolocation' and it can build an incredibly detailed picture of their surroundings. The echo from something far away will take longer to come back and be quieter than something that is closer. Different objects produce different sounds, for example a wall will generate a harsher sound than a leaf, whilst the echo from a mosquito on the move will sound different to that of a dragonfly resting on a twig.

The bats create these sounds themselves, through their voice box, or larynx, which is large and reinforced with bone, and release it through their mouths. They can vary the pitch and tone, the length and intensity of their call, and so refine the images that they pick up. The sound is too high-pitched for humans to hear and is not so much a call as a shout or scream, so loud they would deafen themselves through prolonged exposure. To get around this problem they have developed the ability to turn off their middle ear just before calling, restoring their hearing a split second later so that they can hear the echo.

With each call they build up a constantly evolving picture of what is around them, whether it is moving or stationary, prey or predator. However this is not the only trick up their sleeve. They have sensory receptors in their wings that also read the night. These sensors can identify changes in wind direction or turbulence for example and send a message directly to the brain which results in rapid adjustments to their wing position. Their wings are actually hands that have developed into wings over millions of years from when they were originally flightless, tree-climbing mammals. Each 'hand wing' is extremely flexible and can move independently. As an interesting aside, their scientific name, Chiroptera, is Greek for 'hand wing'.

Put all these characteristics together and it's a winning combination. It needs to be as bats have a prodigious appetite. A common pipistrelle, so small that it could fit into a matchbox, can eat up to 3,000 insects in one night. Luckily for them an enormous number of insects are around at night, providing a plentiful food source and, as most other animals are asleep, there are few competitors to share it with.

Returning briefly, and finally, to the point about bats becoming entangled in hair, there is scientific evidence, of a sort, to prove that there is nothing to fear. Between 1958 and 1961, a man called Gathorne-Hardy, the fifth Earl of Cranbrook and founding member of the Mammal Society, carried out a series of 'experiments' to prove his theory. Using two young ladies as his subjects, one with short hair and one with longer, he placed four different species of bat on their heads and recorded what happened over numerous occasions. Apparently the bats walked about a little and then flew off without disturbing a single hair. And there you have it. Definitive proof. Who could argue with that?

The wood wide web

September is a time for woodland walks, noting how the colour of the leaves are changing and wondering whether they will provide a good display later in the autumn. It's also the time for mushrooms, and I only have to veer off the track a short distance under the canopy before I see them, clustered under the cool damp shade of the trees. Mushroom picking is a popular French tradition, and I often see a man or woman with a basket over their arm, head down as they search for their favourite delicacy. However my interest today lies not so much in what is above the ground as in what is below it.

Mycelium is the part of a mushroom that we can't see, an underground root system that can stretch for hundreds, sometimes thousands, of miles if it were laid out end to end. It doesn't grow in that fashion, however, instead being densely packed and intertwined, a network of cells that are all connected and that function in a very similar way to our human brains, using electrical impulses and electrolytes, albeit on a much larger scale.

This vast subterranean network plays a vital role in the health of the woodlands, breaking down rotting vegetation and recycling it into nutrients like phosphorus and nitrogen, which in turn provide an enriched food source for the trees and other woodland plants. So far, so good, but from here we venture into new territory and it requires an open mind.

I had always assumed that most growing things were passive organisms, naturally programmed to react to the triggers of light and dark, wet and dry, cold and hot, in the very simplest of ways. The notion that trees in particular could communicate with each other seemed to me to be too far-fetched to be true. However, the more I learn about our environment the more I realise that nothing in nature is too far-fetched. The real truth is that all things are possible.

There is now scientific evidence to support the proposal that the mycelium network allows trees to communicate with each other. Mycelium doesn't just grow around tree roots, it actually grows into them, becomes part of them. In doing so trees, and other plants, cease to be singular beings and become part of a potentially vast network. This has come to be described as the wood wide web, similar in concept to our internet, with electrical signals passing from the trees through the fungal grid, a conduit from which they can learn, remember, warn each other of danger, and share food sources. That in itself is startling enough, but the next leap of faith comes in accepting that the trees can alter their behaviour as a result of that information.

As I read this I could feel my eyebrows rising in disbelief, seemingly of their own volition, and despite my best efforts not to be sceptical until I knew all the facts. Even if I could accept that trees could somehow be warned of an impending threat, they were hardly able to move to move themselves out of harm's way. Similarly if one of them was sickening due to a lack of light or poor soil, surely there was nothing that its neighbours could do to save it?

It seems a leap of faith isn't called for as modern science is turning many of our long-held beliefs on their head. Let's look at my first point about trees being a simple, passive species and explain why this is not the case. It might appear that the fungus growing into the tree roots is a parasitic action but in fact this is very much a two-way relationship. Scientists believe 92% of all plants form a connection to the mycelium network and in return they have access to the nutrients, such as phosphorus and nitrogen, that are the by-product of the fungus breaking down rotting matter in the soil. As their part of the bargain, trees and plants will share the by-products of photosynthesis, sugars and carbohydrates, with the mycelium. This is no small commitment as it is estimated that between 40–60% of photosynthates produced by trees are given to the mycelium. Each is providing what the other cannot produce themselves. It has also been proven that nutrients that have been recycled by the mycelium from older trees are redistributed to younger samplings to help them flourish. The system is so interconnected, the varying species so dependent upon each other for sustained growth, that all of them have a vested interest in each other's survival.

My second point related to the sharing of information through the fungal web and I think the best way to explain this is to give specific examples from various research projects. In a greenhouse experiment tomato plants infected with blight sent signals to their healthy neighbours, who in response produced defensive enzymes to help protect them from infection. A tree can release chemicals to make the leaves taste unpleasant when a deer decides to eat them. Similarly, when elms and pines are attacked by leaf-eating caterpillars the tree detects their saliva and recognises them as a threat. They release pheromones to attract parasitic wasps which lay their egg inside the caterpillar, which in turn produces larvae that feed on their caterpillar host. As one tree or plant recognises a threat and reacts to it a warning is passed on and shared over the network, allowing the neighbouring plants to take action. Some responses are relatively quick, others will take time to be effective but trees live a great deal longer than we do and operate on a different timescale to us.

I suspect one of the big questions behind this ever-growing pool of scientific research basically comes down to how you define intelligence generally and communication in particular. No-one is suggesting that trees and their mycelium partner communicate exactly as we do, but there is no doubt that communication is taking place and on a far more sophisticated level than we previously understood. It has long been the human way to judge all other life forms against the baseline of our own brain, but I suspect that viewpoint is beginning to change. I have no doubt that we have much still to learn, about fungi and the mycelium network and also about trees. I make a mental note to myself to revisit this engrossing and complicated topic in five years' time and see how our knowledge has progressed.

There's one problem with that idea. I'm not sure I'll be able to wait that long.

Mary-Jane Houlton

OCTOBER

Autumn leaves, russet and red, a glorious finale

Are owls really wise?

It's ten o'clock at night and the mournful hoot of a tawny owl carries clearly through the still night air. It sounds tantalisingly close, but owls are masters of disguise and I know my chances of seeing it are slim. So often I find myself standing in the field in the dark, peering up at the silhouettes of the branches, and yet I have never seen one, not even a hint of movement as they swoop from one tree to another, nor the slightest whoosh of wings as they fly overhead. I shouldn't be surprised. Most birds have straight-edged flight feathers, which make a sound as air passes over them, but owls have fringed feathers that interlock, eliminating any noise as they fly and making them silent, deadly hunters.

I always associate owls with wisdom, although I have no idea where that belief originated from. I suspect it comes from my childhood, something my parents said, or from fairy tales or children's books and now it is just something I accept without question. But are they really wise?

Those huge eyes and the long, unblinking stare give an impression of a serious nature, one that considers an action and its implications before blindly leaping forth. Whilst there is no doubting that they are incredible hunters, known as 'the wolves of the sky' with some justification, their success is a function of a keen sense of smell and night vision as well as their ability to descend upon their unsuspecting prey on silent wings. They aren't in the same league of intelligence as the problem-solving birds like the corvids and parrots. In fact those huge eyes take up 75% of the space in their skull, so their brain is relatively small compared to other animals.

Throughout the centuries they have been associated with contradicting beliefs, seen as a sign of death or a protector, as wise or foolish, even a portent of victory in battle or a warning of stormy weather. In Greek mythology Athena, goddess of wisdom, chose the owl as her emblem, but in some Indian cultures they are considered stupid birds. They have naturally been seen as creatures of the darkness and with this comes an inherent sense of menace. The fact that they can swivel their heads 270 degrees makes it even easier to believe that there this is something other-worldly about them, but nature is simply being practical. They swivel their heads because their eyes are fixed and so they can only look straight ahead.

With so many conflicting stories about owls I feel no qualms about bequeathing a certain amount of wisdom on what I like to think of as 'my' owls. There is an old nursery rhyme that sums it up perfectly.

The Wise Old Owl

A wise old owl lived in an oak
The more he saw, the less he spoke
The less he spoke, the more he heard
Why can't we all be like that wise old bird?

Slug love

There are some creatures that we find off-putting, somehow disgusting to our human eyes, that make us wrinkle up our noses in distaste. There are others that we deem to be pests, where a constant war is being waged against the background of our passion for growing things and the natural world's unbounded enthusiasm and dedication in consuming the results of our labours.

The slug probably comes top of the list on both those counts: slimy, pulpy, shapeless and with a prodigious appetite. They need to eat twice their own body weight in one day and our gardens provide rich pickings. I knew this to my own personal cost as the first thing I saw this morning was evidence of a good night for my own slug community. I had spent the previous day planting up four pots with chrysanthemums but all that was left was a silvery network of slime trails and bare stems, not a leaf or flower in sight.

Slugs are usually nocturnal. Water makes up most of their body but they're very thin skinned and if they dry out they die, which is why they spend most of their time underground. However, as I walked along our track, grumbling about my lost chrysanthemums under my breath, I couldn't help but notice more slugs than I had ever seen before. These were Spanish slugs (*Arion vulgaris*), and they were scattered in the short grass like swollen, giant-sized pieces of orange-brown confetti, four of five inches in length with stumpy bodies as wide as my finger. There were so many of them I literally had to watch where I put my feet for fear of stepping on one.

I crouched down to get a closer look. Two slugs had joined together, head to head or end to end, making a rough circle. Between them was what I can best describe as a large blob of a bluey-white, glutinous, jelly-type substance.

I wondered if they were dying, or if one was eating the other, but in fact the answer was rather more surprising. The white gooey stuff was a penis. To be accurate it was two penises, one for each slug as they were exchanging sperm. I had stumbled upon the autumn mating season.

I peered more closely but couldn't make out any detail. It still looked like a big blob of rather disgusting jelly. Slugs are hermaphrodites, meaning that they possess both male and female reproductive organs. Some species will self-fertilise, but most slugs will mate with another, and the penis comes from a genital opening on the side of their heads. Each slug can act as the male and exchange sperm internally, or externally, which is what my slugs were doing. Or they can engage in 'simultaneous reciprocal mating' which is where one acts as the male and the other as the female, and they take turns at both roles. Once the mating is over each slug will find a safe place to lay their eggs which will hatch in a month or two.

It's easy to look at another creature, be it animal, insect or bird, and assume that it is a simple organism just because of its size but that is so often not the case. The more I learnt about slugs, the more I found my repulsion replaced by fascination. For example, any gardener knows that slugs leave trails of slime as they move about, but these are not random expulsions. They act as signals and signposts, helping them to return to their tunnels and feeding sites, as well as leaving a scent to attract a mate.

For half an hour I wandered around the field watching slugs, which requires some patience as they don't like to rush things. I knelt down by one that seemed to have stopped by a leaf, and realised that the leaf was moving. Kneeling down closer and zooming in with my camera I could actually see the leaf disappearing, bite by tiny bite, into its mouth. It paused for a second as the camera came close, and then carried on, not at all disturbed by my presence. The leaf was consumed surprisingly quickly, but given that they need to eat such a large amount each day I guess time is of the essence.

I returned to the spot where I had seen that first pair of mating slugs to find that it was all over. They had disappeared and all that remained was a wetly glistening circle of slime.

A few weeks later and the slugs had almost all disappeared. I might see one or two on my walks across the field but nothing compared to the numbers they had been. They had returned to their nocturnal and subterranean world. Slugs breed all year round but peaks of egg-laying occur in March–April and September–October so perhaps I was lucky enough to stumble upon their autumn season of passion.

Water, water everywhere

When we think about transport networks the first examples that typically come into our minds are man-made, primarily road, rail and air. But there is a vast network of streams, rivers and oceans covering the entire planet, interlinked and complex, that provide a very different transport network for the creatures that rely upon them. I stood on a bridge at Lac d'Estaing in the Pyrenees and watched the stream tumbling beneath me as it escaped the calm confines of the lake, such a force of energy, leaping over stones and boulders in its compulsion to move on, to be free. From here it would feed into a network of small streams and rivers, setting off on a journey to who knew where. I wondered what would happen if I were to write a message in a bottle and launch it into these restless waters. Where would it go?

My imaginary bottle would begin its journey in Gave de Labat de Bun, and from there a succession of streams would become rivers, from the Gave de Pau to the much larger Adour River. From here it would be a relatively short hop to Bayonne and the open waters of the Bay of Biscay, giving my bottle the opportunity to cover huge distances, riding on the extensive network of oceans and currents that cover our planet. From Bayonne it might be carried up the west coast of France and into the English Channel, whilst it could even reach the Arctic Ocean after passing Scotland and Norway. From here Greenland beckons, followed by Eastern Canada and the Eastern Seaboard of the United States.

What an epic journey. Alternatively it could get stuck in the roots of a tree or run aground in the shallows before it had even left this valley. A passing walker might pick it up, shaking their head in disgust at the irresponsibility of people who can't be bothered to take their litter home, and throw it in the nearest bin, providing an ignominious end to what might have been such an adventure and my message, whatever it might have been, would never be read.

Messages in bottles have been sent, and some actually received, for centuries. One of the earliest recorded examples was in 310 BC from a Greek philosopher named Theophrastus, a student of Aristotle, who used them to test his theory that the Mediterranean Sea was formed by the inflowing Atlantic Ocean. Rather more dramatically, in 1875 the steward and cabin boy of the British sailing ship *Lennie* released 24 bottles into the Bay of Biscay, with messages telling of how mutineers had killed the ship's captain and officers. They were picked up by the French authorities who came to the rescue and dealt with the ill-fated mutineers.

In 1914, a soldier named Thomas Hughes wrote a letter to his wife, sealed it in a humble ginger ale bottle and threw it into the English Channel. He died two days later. Years passed and in 1999, a fisherman found his bottle in the River Thames. By this time his wife was dead but their daughter, now 86 years old, lived in New Zealand. She had been only a year old when her father died and so never knew him, but the same fisherman who had rescued the bottle travelled to New Zealand and delivered it to her in person.

In 1928, a trapper working on the Agawa River in Ontario rescued a bottle from the water. When he opened it he found the following message: 'I am the last one left alive, freezing and starving to death on Isle Royale in Lake Superior. I just want mom and dad to know my fate.' It had been written by Alice Bettridge, an assistant stewardess on the freighter *Kamloops* which had sunk in a blizzard a year earlier. She had survived the sinking of the boat, but died on the island.

In 1956, the hopes of a Swedish sailor called Ake Viking were answered when he sent a bottled message 'To someone beautiful and far away'. The bottle reached a Sicilian girl and resulted in them getting married in 1958.

I had always regarded the idea of a message in a bottle as little more than a child's game, no different to dropping sticks off one side of the bridge and seeing if they would reappear on the other. History shows that there is so much more to them than that. I was astonished at the sheer volume of accounts where messages in bottles had changed lives, or saved them, or provided a final testament to someone's hopes and fears. These tales, of which those listed above are just a few among the many I could have chosen, illustrate how strange life can be, how it is made up of quirks of chance, or fate, that could never have been foreseen. They show us that life always has the ability to surprise us, to dumbfound us, to bring us to tears or to laughter and, perhaps most crucially of all, they give us a reason to believe in hope and never to give up.

A pointless existence

'What is the point of your existence?' I hissed, slapping futilely at my lower leg a second after a mosquito had just flown off. 'All you do is make life a misery for everybody you come into contact with.'

There are at least 3,500 different species of mosquito and it felt as if most of them had descended upon our valley in the south west of France. It was late October and they shouldn't have been so much of a problem at this time of year but we were having a late Indian summer and these miniature vampires were making the most of it. The female mosquito, not the male, is the guilty party, as blood is rich in proteins and amino acids which she needs for her eggs. She will keep biting and sucking until she is replete or gets disturbed. It's not a pleasant thought but she can fly with two or three times her own body weight of blood on board. She has half a dozen sharp mouthpieces that can easily pierce thin or loosely knit materials and so clothing is not necessarily a barrier.

I strongly believe in live and let live, but I am willing to make an exception for the mosquito. It spreads diseases like malaria, dengue, yellow fever and Zika and kills more people than any other creature in the world. Do they actually make any meaningful contribution? Would they be missed if we could exterminate the lot of them and do we ever have the right to wipe out an entire species?

Dealing with the practical issues before the moral ones, it is unlikely that we could eradicate them. The University of Alaska has a mosquito fossil believed to be 79 million years old, but scientists believe they may have been around for over 200 million years. Either way they are experts at surviving.

Nature has organised itself so that every creature is part of a larger community and has a role to play, even if it is quite simply to be eaten or to eat, to kill or be killed. Like everything else mosquitoes are part of the food chain and feasting on our blood is not their only purpose in life. In fact only around 10% of them feed on humans and other animals. In the wider sense they are pollinators, particularly the males, who prefer plant nectar to blood. Their larvae provide food for fish and as adults they are preyed upon by birds, bats and frogs. It's not possible to say definitively one way or the other whether there would be anything as catastrophic as a population collapse in these other species if the mosquito were to suddenly disappear but we have no means of getting rid of them anyway so for the moment the question is irrelevant.

I find it ironic that we have so much technology at our fingertips, and yet we are powerless against this tiny, ancient insect. We can fight back with repellent sprays, with screens, with thick clothing, getting rid of any stagnant water in our gardens, and yet we can't beat them. The mosquito has the last laugh.

Is it morally right to wish an entire species dead because, at best, it is an inconvenience and, at worst, it can kill me? Whether right or wrong, we have a long history of killing things that stand in our way. It seems to be part of our nature but I think there is a question of degree. Killing creatures just because they inconvenience us is too extreme. With greater knowledge and understanding we can alter our perceptions and our response to the problem.

I pulled out a bottle of eucalyptus insect repellent and sprayed it liberally over my legs, face and arms and acknowledged that my opinion on this particular pest hadn't changed, despite a strong belief in tolerance and understanding. I still fervently wished that we were free of them. For now, sadly, there was nothing to do but put up with it.

NOVEMBER

Woolly hats and warm gloves, winter creeps in on the

morning mist

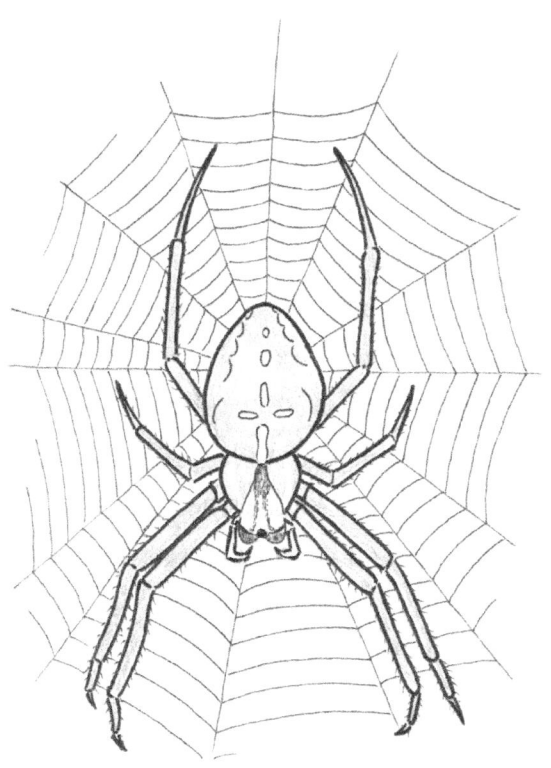

Can we make things better?

I am more than three-quarters of the way through my year of asking questions and I can see that my perception and understanding of my immediate environment has changed. Now that I know more about the wildlife around me I feel increasingly protective about them and have a greater sense of responsibility for their welfare. This is a change for the good but it is set against a distressing backdrop, given an ever-increasing amount of research and statistical data which shows so many species are struggling to survive.

Scientists are suggesting that we are entering the sixth mass extinction. There are various theories about what exactly caused the previous five extinctions, a combination of factors such as unstable temperatures, the planet being hit by an asteroid or suffering the after-effects of a volcanic eruption. However there is a growing body of evidence to support the proposition that homo sapiens is responsible for this latest extinction. The Earth is 4.5 billion years old, the human race has been around for a mere 200,000 years, and yet in that relatively short time our expanding population and the way we live have fundamentally altered the physical, chemical and biological systems on which we and all other organisms depend.

During the past 60 years the speed and the scale of the change has accelerated and this figure hits hard because it has happened within my lifetime. We have plundered the land through a combination of agriculture, logging, hunting and fishing; our cities and other settlements, plus the vast and invasive infrastructure we have developed to support our ever-growing needs, pollute our waterways and clog up the very air we breathe. We have taken the lion's share of the bounty that this Earth has offered us and the wild creatures have suffered as a result.

How many have we lost already and how many are on the brink? Given that we don't know how many species there were on the planet in the first place, it's no simple matter to give an accurate figure on how many have disappeared or are under threat. To some extent it depends on where you take your baseline, where that first measurement stems from, and even then it will vary from country to country, region to region, year to year. The statistics are continually in a state of flux. It should also be pointed out that extinction is a natural phenomenon, historically happening slowly over hundreds, even thousands, of years. This gradual process gives time for other species to evolve and for nature to replace what has been lost, maintaining the balance within the ecosystem. Crucially that is no longer the case. The number of extinctions each year is now far in excess of what they would be if humans were not on the planet, almost as if someone has pressed the fast-forward button on the movie of life on Earth and we are hurtling forwards, out of control.

What can we do? Will we learn and make some attempt to atone for our mistakes or are we set on a path from which there is now no going back?

I look back over my past chapters and the animals and birds that have become companions to me and wonder at their status, whether they are in decline or doing well. It's easy to be overcome by despair, to always assume the worst, but I am looking for hope, for some proof that humanity can be a force for good. I found an example of how we have fought to protect and retain the species that we still have in the story of the kingfisher.

It is unusual to have such a brightly coloured bird in the UK and their beauty became part of their downfall during the late 1800s. Their feathers were used for fishing flies, their eggs became collectors' items and the birds were stuffed and placed under glass as an ornament in fine town and country houses. They were also prized as a fashion item in ways that are hard to understand all these years later. Women of high society wore feathers, wings or even whole birds to adorn their hats, stoles and dresses.

A group of women in Manchester were so horrified at the mass slaughter of birds for so meaningless a thing as a fashion fad that they took a stand against it, forming a protest group called the Plumage League in 1889. Their first leaflet concentrated on the egret population, enlightening women as to the harsh reality behind their fashion accessory. In 1902 a London auction house sold around 1,600 packages of heron and egret feathers. Each package used the feathers of 120 birds, meaning that over 190,000 birds were killed to satisfy demand, and this figure is from just one supplier amongst many. Plume hunters recognised a business opportunity and ruthlessly exploited it, travelling the world to satisfy the London and European feather markets, their prey any birds that were without protection, including the kingfisher amongst many others: parrots, eagles, owls, hummingbirds, grebes, starlings, magpies, pheasants, birds of paradise – the list goes on and on.

The Plumage League joined forces with another protest group, the Fur, Fin and Feather Folk, and by 1898 they had 20,000 members. Today the association has over a million members, making it one of the world's largest conservation organisations, and we know it as the Royal Society for the Protection of Birds (RSPB). They are not alone. The WWF (World Wide Fund for Nature) has over five million supporters and works to protect species and their habitats in more than 100 countries and there are many others, some working at an international levels, others more locally. Friends of the Earth has over two million members, and Greenpeace is supported by three and a half million people. Without organisations such as these to fight on behalf of animals the situation would be even worse than it is.

It is possible to bring animals back from the brink of extinction, or to boost population numbers, if we can protect both them and their habitats by law. For example, the kingfisher is protected under the Wildlife and Countryside Act in the UK, making it illegal to kill or injure a bird and their chicks, or damage or disturb their nests. Badgers, bats, otters and hares are amongst many other species who gain some protection through international legislation.

It gives some solace to know that there are millions of

people out there who care about animals and will support these organisations, both financially and through volunteer work. However it doesn't change the bleak reality and every day there are new headlines in the press drawing attention to another species on the decline. The RSPB states that 38 million birds have disappeared from our skies in the last 50 years. One of the most recent reports from the CMS (Convention on the Conservation of Migratory Species of Wild Animals) found 44% of species that they monitored are in decline, with 22% threatened with extinction. Every global conservation organisation has their own set of statistics and whilst the percentages and types of survey may vary, the message remains the same. The natural world is in crisis and whilst it is true that conservation really can make a difference, it's an uphill struggle.

What about me? It's one thing to ask what the human race in general can do to make things better, but what am I doing? Michael and I live a simple life off-grid for much of the time, so that our carbon footprint is as low as we can make it, and we manage our field so that it provides a good environment for the wildlife, but I have gained a new awareness since I started asking my questions over this year and I feel that I am not doing enough. How I should act upon this feeling is not yet clear but it will be an important question to ponder over the coming winter.

Flight of the spiderlings

Something brushed across my cheek. Just the lightest of touches, so delicate that it only registered on the margins of my conscious thought. It was mid-morning and I had climbed up through the woods and was walking along the quiet tarmac road that runs along the spine of the hill above Le Shack. Green fields stretched away on either side of me, empty of cattle until the summer returned. There were no people and no cars, just me, quite alone.

There it was again. I ran my hand over my face but could find nothing to explain it. It felt as if I had walked into a spider's web but, given the open nature of the landscape, that made no sense.

And then I saw them, almost as if the mere act of thinking the words had opened my eyes to what was all around me. Not spiders' webs, but single strands of spider's silk, looking like bits of a web that had broken off. The wind was blowing gently across the top of the hill, from one side of the road to the other, and there were dozens and dozens of silvery gossamer threads twinkling in the sunshine, some short, some long, reminding me strangely of the Lametta tinsel strands I used to spend hours hanging on the branches of our Christmas tree as a child. As I walked on the silk caught on my jacket, silver on black, and I could see where it had snagged on the barbed wire fences. The strands that had been lifted higher by the wind and so had avoided any obstacles were the longest, stretching three feet or more. I stopped and focused on one of them, trying to predict its flight path, wondering whether there was some purpose to this rather beautiful phenomenon.

Everyone knows that spiders spin their silk to trap prey, creating a clever device that acts both as a home and a source of food. Until that morning I had not realised that they also used silk as a means of transport. These individual strands, or draglines, allow the spider to ride the wind from one location to the other, a technique known as 'ballooning'. It is a common way for young spiders, known as 'spiderlings', to disperse from their nest. They will travel to a high point, raise their abdomens, which is where they manufacture their silk, and release one or more strands. The wind and thermal currents bear them aloft, flying free into the great unknown. I screwed up my eyes, hoping to see a tiny spiderling at one end of a strand, but they were constantly moving, rising and falling with the air currents. If there was a passenger aboard, I could see no sign of it, but what a wonderful way to begin anew, casting yourself to the wind and letting it take you where it will. I was looking at a fleet of silken sails, a veritable armada of spiders.

It's hard to believe that these small creatures have the ability to produce as much as 20 metres of silk every day. The silk has different properties depending on its primary purpose, whether it be sticky so that it traps prey or particularly elastic and strong if used as a structural attachment for the web itself. Yet another type of silk is used for swathing their prey once they have caught it and another is used to make protective egg sacs.

The largest spider web found to date spans a river in the Andasibe-Mantadia National Park in Madagascar. It is suspended above the water on 80-foot-long anchor lines which the spider feeds out across the water until they catch on the trees and undergrowth on the far side. A huge orb web, which can be up to 30 feet square, is then spun at the central point.

It would be easy to assume that the spider who can spin such a gigantic web would be a monster of its species, an arachnophobe's worst nightmare, but in fact Darwin's bark spider, which was only discovered in 2009, is no more than an inch long, cleverly camouflaged in dull tones that allow it to merge into the bark of a tree.

An hour or so later I arrived back at Le Shack and made a point of noticing the spider webs that were a common sight in the long grass in our field, so wonderfully intricate, but typically no more than four or five inches at their widest point. I simply couldn't imagine one as wide as five feet, almost as tall as I am. It would have taken an incredible amount of patience and tenacity to build and maintain such a structure and I found myself humbled by the realisation that such a tiny creature could aspire to something so grandiose. There is so much that the natural world can teach us, valuable life lessons to be learnt if we keep our eyes open. I watched a small insect that had unwittingly flown into a web being efficiently despatched by the resident arachnid and resolved not to judge any creature, human or otherwise, by their outward appearance or size. Perhaps we are all capable of more than we realise.

A day of gifts

It's strange how quickly memories of summer become distant. It happens every year and still always takes me by surprise. The transition to autumn isn't always easy: moving from long sunny days to long dark nights, from living in shorts and t-shirts to bundling up in fleeces, from feeling that the weather is a benign force to a sense that it can be antagonistic. At this time of year a sunny day after prolonged grey skies is a precious gift and not a minute can be wasted.

Our day of gifts this week was a Wednesday in early November, a brief interlude of sunshine amongst days of rain, and so we headed to the Pyrenees, a drive of around one and a half hours from our cabin. So often Michael and I walk by ourselves, two pairs of walking boots following the trail. We enjoy our own company, the ease of being quiet together, the freedom to choose our own pace. Today we were with friends who knew the mountains better than we did, our private tour guides. The dynamics of walking changes when there are four pairs of walking boots instead of two and if one is lucky, as we were, the sum can turn out to be greater than the value of its parts. There is something about the simple act of putting one foot in front of the other that allows conversations to meander down paths that you might not otherwise follow. There are different perspectives and opinions to be shared, different things to laugh at, and a common bond in knowing that there was something about being in these mountains that moved us all.

The first snow was appearing on the higher slopes and so we picked a walk in the foothills, beginning at the Chapel de Houndas, climbing gently along well-marked trails, our goal the standing stones of Lous Couraus. So often in these mountains the trails are stony and steep and I find myself walking with my head down, picking my path with care, oblivious to all that surrounds me. However this was one of those days where the landscape demanded that I stop and pay homage. I paused and looked back down the way I had just come, a patchwork of trails cutting their way through the rich chestnut colour of the bracken.

Turning slowly full circle I followed the line of the mountains as they swept up from the valley floor. The trees had been lulled into a false sense of security by the extended summer and were still green and lush for the most part, the merest hint of gold and rust giving a token nod to autumn. In the far distance the jagged peaks of the highest summits knew that winter was coming and had donned their winter mantles in preparation, the new snowfall glinting in the sunshine.

Lower down the valley the silence was broken by the excited barking of dogs and the clanging of cow bells. A few minutes later a small herd of honey-coloured cattle appeared on the trail behind us, the heavy bells around their necks ringing out a bovine anthem in praise of clean mountain air and good grazing. Three farm mutts came hard on their heels, yipping, yapping and so beside themselves with excitement that they spooked the cattle, sending half of them off in the wrong direction. Behind them came the farmer, shouting in exasperation at his dogs to do their job and bring the herd back together. As they passed us by and the clanging, barking and shouting faded away, the silence filled the spaces again, settling down with a contented sigh.

Higher and higher we climbed. We stopped for lunch at the stone circles, peeling off layers and stretching out on the grass in the unexpectedly warm midday sunshine, tucking into our egg sarnies with the enthusiasm that always comes after a hike up a hill. There were in fact 16 different stone circles, but they were so small and so haphazardly placed that if we had been looking in any other direction we could have missed them entirely. A noticeboard informed us that they had been there for around 3,000 years, their exact purpose never discovered. Perhaps they had been placed there simply to provide a focal point for people to meet, to enjoy the view and commune with the mountains. It worked for us.

I sensed a shadow passing over my head, a prickle of warning from predator to prey, and above me a griffon vulture floated effortlessly. Soon there were five of them, flying so low that I could make out their long, scrawny white necks and the serrated edges of their wings with my naked eye. Keen for more detail, I grabbed the binoculars and tilted my head back, following them as they circled around us, marvelling at how the slightest adjustment of those impressive wings, with an average span of two and a half metres, allowed them to catch the thermals, consummate masters of the skies. Each feather must have had its part to play, a tiny but vital contribution to the whole, and I wondered how many feathers a bird of prey like this would have.

The answer is typically between 5,000 to 8,000, a figure that relates to all the large birds of prey, not just vultures. A blackbird has between 1,500 to 3,000, a chicken around 8,000, whilst a swan can have as many as 25,000 feathers.

Feathers are wondrous things, lightweight and insubstantial and yet so cleverly designed that they allow birds to fly thousands of miles as they migrate from continent to continent. They hold a hummingbird in place as it feeds on nectar, enable the humble sparrow to dive into the undergrowth to evade the hawk, and allow swallows to feed on the wing.

However there is so much more to feathers than providing the means of flight. They repel rain and protect the bird from the heat of the sun. Down feathers, lying close to the skin, provide insulation and in winter birds will fluff their feathers up, creating an air space between them, to keep themselves warm. The colour of the feathers also has a part to play, in some cases acting as camouflage so that the bird blends into the environment whilst in others it does the opposite and a colourful plumage is flaunted to attract a mate.

I used to collect feathers as a child, finding them simply a thing of beauty and content to judge them on that alone, but now I wish I had known more. If I had appreciated the range of tasks they performed, from helping the bird to fly and to feed, to providing a coat that protected them in all weathers and temperatures, and that hid them from predators as well as attracting a mate, I would have held my collection of feathers in even higher regard.

'I wonder what they're thinking about as they fly up so high?' I mused, putting the binoculars away and rubbing the back of my neck, which had developed a crick in it from staring skyward for too long. 'Do they enjoy the sun on their backs? Do they ever fly just for the joy of it?'

I could see why people would make the assumption that birds wouldn't have much of a brain, particularly the smaller of the species. There simply isn't much space for a brain in those tiny skulls but research, particularly more recent research, has shown that size is not the only factor to take into account. Some species, ravens and crows in particular, have shown signs of intelligence and an ability to learn, to communicate, and to relate to humans.

The diminutive goldcrest, weighing approximately one tenth as much as a mouse, has twice as many brain cells. It's not just the size of the brain that counts but how densely it is packed with neurons and this is what determines the level of intelligence. For a long time it was believed that birds didn't have a cerebral cortex, the source of intelligence in our human brains, but we know now that they have a similar structure, known as a 'pallium', and that it has some striking similarities to our cortex.

One wonders how scientists glean all this information. A woman called Suzana Herculano-Houzel, working with a team of fellow scientists at the university in Rio de Janeiro, developed an instrument called an isotropic fractionator. It sounds like a time travel machine, but it actually counts brain cells. A brain is soaked in paraformaldehyde, making it easier to cut into identifiable sections, and then dissolved in a salty detergent, effectively turning it into a cloudy soup. Drops of this liquid brain are placed within the isotropic fractionator and counted. Herculano-Houzel and her team have compared the brains of 28 different bird species and their findings have shown that song birds and parrots have brains that are much bigger relative to their body size than some small monkeys.

We use the term 'bird brain' as an insult, inferring that someone is stupid or scatterbrained, but it appears that we are doing our feathered friends an injustice. Size isn't everything and you don't have to be big to be clever.

Pot of gold

My father always told my brother and me that there was a pot of gold at the end of the rainbow when we were children and for years we believed him. If my memories are to be trusted it mostly happened whilst we were out driving in the car and we would squeal in delight as he followed the rainbow trail to a nearby hill or a copse of trees. Of course the rainbow is a trickster, a fleeting band of colour that played games with us, always just out of reach, always moving on, and we never found our pot of gold. That disappointment never dulled our enthusiasm, the naïve childish belief in a pleasing tale standing firm against reality.

On rainy days at Le Shack I might see a rainbow as I look out of the kitchen window and across the valley. The other day one clearly ended in a copse of trees just below the cabin and a small, childish part of me was tempted to forget about making soup and charge out across the field in search of a cauldron filled with gold nuggets. Sadly my adult mind stepped in and quashed such a ridiculous notion before I could get out of the door.

The rainbows are real, a ribbon of many hues formed when sunlight is scattered from raindrops, but the pot of gold is a myth. According to Irish folklore, leprechauns would often bury their gold at the end of a rainbow. If you were lucky enough to catch one of these grumpy, bearded faerie-goblins they might grant you three wishes in exchange for their release but persuading them to share their gold was no easy task. They hoarded it fiercely, and had a reputation for being treacherous. Great care had to be taken in choosing your three wishes or you might get something you hadn't bargained for.

In 1989 an Irish publican called P J O'Hare claimed that he had found the remains of a leprechaun in Carlingford, County Louth. The skeleton crumbled to dust but he kept the clothes and displayed them in his pub. A group of leprechaun enthusiasts claim that only 236 of them remain in Ireland and all of them live in Carlingford. As a result of their lobbying efforts leprechauns have been protected by a European directive since 2009. Finding this hard to believe I plunged into the official website for the Habitats Directive, which protects wild animals, plants and habitats in Europe and, whilst I learnt that there are protective plans in place for the common midwife toad and the Danube clouded yellow butterfly, I could find no reference to the elusive leprechaun. Given the extensive nature of the website they could have been hidden away in any number of lists and locations and so I will give the leprechaun fans the benefit of the doubt.

Each year these enthusiasts gather for a leprechaun hunt in Carlingford, as do other groups dotted about through Europe and America. Strangely enough, no live leprechauns have ever been found, but the strategic placement of doll-like replicas along the trail ensures that the hunt is always a success.

It would be all too easy to dismiss these enthusiasts as being eccentric, but on the other hand I find our willingness to believe in things other than ourselves, no matter how whimsical or ridiculous, to be something to celebrate. Instead of viewing it with a cynical eye, we could decide that the ability to indulge in flights of fancy is one of the better characteristics of the human race and certainly a welcome relief from the prejudice and bitterness that threatens to engulf us all at the moment.

As I peeled and chopped my carrots and parsnips, and the rainbow across the valley faded gently away, I imagined a leprechaun, clothed in red and green, a jaunty hat perched atop his head, crouched over his gold in the undergrowth in that copse of trees down the hill. Perhaps he was looking up at me, a knowing glint in his eye, secure in the knowledge that as long as I didn't really believe in him both he and his gold were safe.

Mary-Jane Houlton

DECEMBER

Log fires, candles burning, curtains drawn,

inward turning

Head in the clouds

Michael hunkered down in front of the woodburner. I was still in bed, hanging on to that drowsy in-between state of half-awake, half-asleep. There had been a hard frost overnight and the air in our cabin was cold against my cheeks. Lighting the fire first thing in the morning was a ritual and I didn't need to look at him to know exactly what he was doing. The kindling caught quickly, the flames bringing a warm glow to the room and the illusion of instant heat, a state of mind rather than a reality. It would take time before the cabin was properly warmed up.

I propped myself up against my pillows, cup of tea in my hands, and watched the sun as it touched the tops of the trees. One of the most satisfying things about living in such a tiny home, with everything in one room, is that I can enjoy my morning cup of tea in bed in front of the fire whilst Michael sits at the table, only a few feet away, eating his breakfast, perusing the news and sharing any interesting headlines with me. In a conventional house where all the rooms are separated by walls this admirable arrangement doesn't work.

Sadly, this morning ritual is not what it once was. The media these days seems fixed on presenting us with bad news and I mourn the loss of a time when they still managed to find a few good things to share.

I sighed. It was going to be a perfect day, far too good to

stay in bed thinking gloomy thoughts about the state of the world. I swung my legs out from beneath the duvet, wincing as my feet touched the cold floorboards. Thermals, fleece and warm trousers were hastily pulled on and a second cup of tea was poured. Wellie boots were donned and I grabbed a hat on the way out. It was going to be a blue sky day, wall to wall winter sunshine. I love blue skies. They make me happy and never fail to lift my spirits.

Why is the sky blue? At sunrise and sunset it can be any number of other colours: orange and red, pink and purple. I thought about it for a moment, expecting an answer to materialise from somewhere, and then realised I had no idea. The sky was just there, a part of my world that I took for granted and never questioned.

Our light comes from the sun. Before it reaches Earth's atmosphere it appears white, even though it contains all the hues and tones of the colour spectrum. As that white light hits the molecules contained in our atmosphere it splits, the individual colours scattered in many different directions. Each colour reacts differently according to their wavelengths, which is where the science starts to get more complicated, but to put it simply the blue light is dominant during daylight hours, which is why we see a blue sky. At sunrise and sunset, when the sun is lower in the sky, the light has a longer distance to travel through our atmosphere, leading to orange and red colours becoming stronger.

There are actually two reasons which explain why we see a blue sky. The first relates to the scattering effect described above, but the other reason relates the physiology of human vision. Physics tells us that sky is not the pure blue that we believe it to be, but rather a mix of violet and blue which tends towards purple. Our eyes are more sensitive to detecting blue light, however, and so that is what we pick up on. Outside of humans and some primates, most animals have a different cone structure in their eyes and they will see something different to us. We are all looking at the same thing and yet we have different realities.

I looked at the sky above me, slightly awestruck at the revelation that it wasn't quite what it seemed. Squinting, I tried to find a hint of violet within the blue but it remained elusive. The buzzards were circling above the woods, as they so often did, and I wondered what colour their sky was.

Fluffy white clouds were crowding in from the west and before I knew it a new question popped into my head. Why are clouds white? Or grey or black?

The answer lies in the size of the rain droplets held in the cloud. They are larger than the molecules in the atmosphere, which means that all colours are scattered equally and so the sunlight remains in its original white state. This creates the effect of a white cloud against the blue sky. When light is scattered in a cloud it moves up, or out, to the sides and top of the cloud and so these areas will appear the whitest. The density of these water droplets will dictate how much sunlight gets through and so will affect the colour of the cloud. The denser the particles, the darker the clouds will appear, ranging from grey to black. This is particularly noticeable as we stand on Earth, looking up at the bottom of clouds, the area which receives the least amount of light.

There is a society or club for most things in life and so it is with clouds. The Cloud Appreciation Society came into being almost by accident. In 2004 a man called Gavin Pretor-Pinney gave a talk on clouds at a literature festival in the UK, with the title of 'The inaugural lecture of the Cloud Association Society'. In fact there was no society; the title was tongue-in-cheek, a device to promote interest, but his talk was so well received that people asked if they could join. As of September 2023 the society has 60,000 members from 120 countries.

In June 2013 he gave a Ted Talk with another catchy title, 'Cloudy with a chance of joy'. He made the point that clouds often have negative connotations, being associated with phrases like 'under a cloud' or 'clouds on the horizon'. So often we see them as something that blocks out the sun and spoils our day. Often we don't even notice them at all, regarding them as too commonplace, too mundane, and yet this lack of awareness is to our great loss.

As his talk progressed I had a flashback to my childhood, passing the time on long car journeys by gazing out of the window and imagining castles and dragons in the clouds. I spent much of my time day-dreaming as a young girl, losing myself in made-up worlds, stories and images tumbling around in my head, my imagination running free. It doesn't happen so much these days.

Gavin Pretor-Pinney made the point that lying on our backs and watching the clouds is good for our souls, giving us an excuse to slow down, and that living with your head in the clouds helps you keep your feet on the ground. Wise words indeed.

The moon of the long night

It's 10pm, we are entrenched in the depths of winter and the temperatures are close to freezing. On such a night it can be hard to drag myself away from a warm fire but our composting loo at Le Shack is outside, and so there is little choice in the matter.

When we lived in a conventional house, one with the long-forgotten luxury of an inside loo, we shut the doors and drew the curtains when night fell, mostly venturing out again only when the sun rose the next day. Those mysterious hours of darkness were another world, one where I never felt particularly comfortable, my over-active imagination conjuring up any number of dangers lurking in the shadows.

We bought Le Shack just over four years ago and I have become accustomed to making this short nocturnal walk to the loo, which is housed in a small shed a few metres away from the cabin. Strangely, it has become precious in a way that I never expected. I have seen first-hand how the world does indeed become very different at night, and I have learnt to embrace that difference, no longer finding it something to be wary of.

As soon as I set foot out of the door I lift my eyes skyward and of their own volition they search out Orion's Belt, a habit that I am hardly aware of, and from there my gaze roams at will, skimming over the Plough, always on the lookout for shooting stars. After a few seconds my night vision kicks in and it's as if a veil lifts. As each minute passes more and more stars peek out from the rich, velvety darkness, pin-pricks of diamond light. Each one is sharp and clearly defined as we are hidden away in the French countryside, with no light pollution from towns or cities to obscure our view. I see this celestial display night after night and my sense of wonder never dims, shining as bright as the stars themselves.

The silence feels close and comforting, not threatening. Occasionally it will be broken by the mournful hoot of an owl, perhaps a fox or deer barking. The field rises gently up the hill and on a clear night with a full moon I can see almost all of it, the terrain so familiar to me, and yet somehow it becomes other-worldly when bathed in moonlight.

It's easy to believe in fairies and goblins on such nights. Witches and werewolves are creatures of the dark and whilst we sleep they roam. In times past they believed that the full moon caused people to go mad. The Roman goddess of the moon was called Luna, and from that came 'lunatic'. In 18th century England people on trial for murder would ask for a lighter sentence on the grounds of lunacy committed under a full moon. It's hard to believe that a judge would see that as a mitigating circumstance, but if you transported a person from that age into our world there would be much that they found equally outlandish.

I had always assumed that the full moon lasted a day, perhaps two days if you take one on the wax and one on the wane, and to the naked eye this certainly seems to be the case, but the moon is in constant motion around the Earth and so a true full moon is fleeting, and lasts for only an instant. We get a full moon every 29.5 days and because the cycle of the moon doesn't exactly match our calendar month there are some years when we get 13 full moons instead of the usual 12. That extra moon is always called a blue moon, although why it is given that name is a mystery as the colour doesn't change from the usual shade of grey-white.

On that particular December night I was looking up at the Cold Moon, or the Long Night Moon. The full moon has a different name each month. Many of these names are English adaptations from Native American language, whilst others have their roots in Celtic, Anglo-Saxon or pagan traditions. As a result, each full moon has not one name, but many names, although they seem to have one thing in common. They reflect a connection to the cycles of the natural world, and describe how the lives of the humans and animals that seek to find shelter and food on this Earth are governed by those seasons. As you read through just a small selection of the names for the full moon that I have compiled below, you may find, as I did, that they are lyrical, beguiling in their simplicity and redolent of a different era. It was a time when humans were familiar with the habits of wolves and bears, when they grew their own food and understood that a hard winter or a poor harvest could be a matter of life and death.

January / Wolf Moon

This refers to the howling of hungry wolves in deepest winter when food may be scarce. Other names are Stay Home Moon and Quiet Moon.

February / Snow Moon

Named after abundant snowfall. Also known as Hungry Moon and Bear Moon, the latter because bear cubs are born in the winter months.

March / Worm Moon

Describes the worms coming out of the soil as the land warms. Also known as the Crow Moon as the crows are returning, or the Lenten Moon for Anglo Saxons as spring is on the way. In Old English it was called the Chaste Moon to reflect the purity of the season.

April / Pink Moon

In North America this is the time when the pink phlox comes into flower. Also known as the Moon of the Red Grass Appearing. The Celts called it the Budding Moon or the New Shoots Moon.

May / Flower Moon

Another reference to the spring. Also known as Bright Moon or Grass Moon.

June / Strawberry Moon

This relates to berries ripening. The Celts called it Horse Moon (I'm not sure why) or Rose Moon.

July / Buck Moon

New antlers are emerging on the deer. Also known as Salmon Moon, or Thunder Moon.

August / Sturgeon Moon

The Great Lakes are teeming with fish at this time of year, an essential source of food for the Native American tribes. The Anglo Saxons named it the Grain Moon for much the same reason.

September / Harvest Moon

A time of year to take the bounty of the long summer and lay down stocks for the winter. Also known as Corn Moon or Barley Moon.

October / Hunter's Moon

A time for hunting, slaughtering and preserving meat. Also known as the Harvest Moon, or Falling Leaves Moon or Freezing Moon.

November / Beaver Moon

The beavers are also preparing for winter. Other names include Frost Moon, or Darkest Depths Moon.

December / Cold Moon

The name says it all, but another option is the Long Night Moon.

Our modern culture and society, particularly in the westernised world, has changed beyond recognition from the world depicted in these ancient names. Most of us find our food in supermarkets, choosing from thousands of products sourced from all around the world, and we are blissfully unaware of whether harvests have been good or poor because there will always be another producer or another country which can fill the gap. All we see is a packet on the shelf and we have no idea of the story behind it. In many ways this is progress. It is a blessing to be spared the whims of nature and climate and the devastating effect they can have on the food supply chain but it is something that can too easily be taken for granted. We have created an intricate, yet increasingly fragile, web of supply and demand and grown complacent on an illusion of security.

As I stand in the field and look up at the Long Night Moon, I feel in my heart that we have lost something precious. Our connection to the natural world grows ever weaker, important skills and knowledge now lost. We can't turn the clock back but I'm wary of what the future holds. A clock is ticking somewhere and I feel the need to strengthen my own connection to the natural world, to grab every opportunity and appreciate it fully. And so, as ridiculous as it might sound, I am grateful for this nightly ritual to the loo, for without it I would have remained closeted inside my four walls. I would have never thought to question the names of the moon and what they mean.

As we settle down for the night and turn the lights off, the full moon shines in brightly, a comforting reminder that times have indeed changed but she has not. She is as she always was and will be back again in another 29.5 days. As I drift off to sleep my last waking thought is that I should compile my own list of names for the moon, a personal reflection on this modern world and my place within it. I wonder what those ancient civilisations would make of such a list.

The first snowman

Five pieces of coal, a carrot and a scarf are lying on the lawn. Nobody put them on the lawn but there is a perfectly logical reason why they are there. What is it?

This simple riddle brought to mind a memory of childhood days, rolling snow into a ball with great excitement and tenderly creating my first snowman. I picked out a few bits of coal from the scuttle, sneaked a carrot from the cupboard and arranged my scarf around his neck, the finishing touch that brought a smile to his face, although not so much for my mother as it had been a Christmas present and was not intended to be left outside in all weathers. My snowman didn't last long and I can still remember my disappointment when I came down one morning and all that was left was the carrot and coal on the grass.

Making snowmen has long been a favourite game for children, but in times past they were more of an art form for adults to enjoy. The first illustration depicting a snowman dates back to 1380, but there is a belief that they had been around before then, perhaps back to our ancestors and the age of Neanderthal man. Certainly our fascination spans many cultures and countries. A young Michelangelo, 19 years old, was commissioned by the ruler of Florence to sculpt a snowman in his courtyard in 1494.

In more modern times the snowman plays a key role at Zurich's spring festival. He is known as the *Böögg*, which roughly translates as 'bogeyman', and each year he is paraded through the town, a giant snowman, his body stuffed with straw and his head crammed with firecrackers. At the end of the parade he is placed on a pyre and when he finally explodes winter is officially over. Tradition has it that the faster the flames reach his head, the warmer the summer will be.

Japan's famous Sapporo Snow Festival is a celebration of all things icy and snowy, with one of their displays being a colony of thousands of miniature snowmen, standing in a field or on a ledge of ice, lined up in ranks, each with a message from their creator pinned to their cold chests.

There was no sign of any snow at Le Shack on this particular winter's day. Under clear skies we can just see the Pyrenees but, even at this distance, it is obvious that snow is becoming scarcer each year. Apparently snow doesn't often come to these valleys and certainly we haven't seen any in our time here which is a shame. My childhood days are long gone but I think I still have enough of the child buried deep inside who would relish the chance to build another snowman. I suspect that with the way the climate is changing it is not to be, and I will have to content myself with my memories.

Holly

'Ow! That hurt.' A drop of blood welled up from my finger. 'Whose stupid idea was this?'

Unfortunately there was no-one to blame but myself. I was out in the woods, on a mission to collect a few sprigs of holly for Christmas. The best branches, those most heavily laden with bright scarlet berries, were tucked in the middle of a thicket some way off the track. I'd fought my way in through a tangle of brambles and paid the price, but eventually I emerged triumphant, five or six beautiful long stems clutched in a slightly bloodied hand.

I had cut these stems in a bid to cheer myself up in a month when the natural world can seem bleak. I might choose to bring some holly into the home simply for colour but in times past it was thought to protect the household from malevolent fairies and was a charm against witches, goblins and the devil himself. A holly hedge was particularly useful as it provided an effective barrier against any local witches who might feel an urge to run along the top of it, although why they should feel the need to do this was hard to understand. Given that they could far more easily hop on a broomstick, the logic behind the hedge myth seemed flawed.

The more I become acquainted with folklore and legends of times past, the more I realise that our predecessors lived in an era both blessed and cursed. Their lack of knowledge allowed imagination to run wild, creating wonderful stories, inventing gods and demons, seeing signs and significant manifestations in the simplest of things, building a set of beliefs that we scoff at in our supposedly enlightened age. Regrettably, there was also a darker side, one of the most infamous being women burnt at the stake for witchcraft. We have gained much from creating a new digital age, all-seeing, all-knowing, but we have also lost something I think. Perhaps life becomes rather dull when fairytales and ancient beliefs become meaningless.

Holly trees were traditionally planted near to houses to protect from lightning, a tradition based on a connection with Thor, the god of thunder. Many years later, science has shown that the spines on holly leaves can act as miniature lightning conductors. Perhaps we shouldn't be too quick to dismiss old wives' tales after all.

Winter larder

I've always had a soft spot for squirrels. Others might regard them as pests, but I find them endearing, always perky, always busy. One of the reasons they are so industrious is because food can be scarce in winter and it's a full-time job to amass a store large enough to see them through. Many animals have a larder, hidden away in a safe place, but the squirrel has hundreds of store cupboards, with nuts from a wide variety of trees stashed all over their territory. One of their favourite spots is at the entrance to our field and I regularly see evidence of their activities in the disturbed soil and leaves.

This type of behaviour is known as 'scatter hoarding' and one of the motives behind it is to protect against other animals stealing their food. Squirrels seem obsessed at holding on to their supplies, digging up and reburying them many times and even digging fake holes to fool an onlooker with theft on their mind. Quality control is a serious business and as each nut is collected it is shaken to test for weevils. Should the nut be infested it is eaten immediately, together with the unfortunate weevils, as it won't last the season.

With so many small hoards of nuts spread over a large area, it would be easy to assume that the squirrel would forget where many of them are, but their memory is highly spatially aware and they have a good sense of smell. Those few that they do misplace will germinate into a new generation of trees and a future food source. As usual, nature has it all sorted out.

Another resident of our field is the mole. We have so many molehills that I have visions of an army of them down there, digging away manically on some personal mission to turn our little patch of land into an ankle-twisting assault course for humans. However one mole covers a large territory and has a prodigious appetite, consuming its own body weight in earthworms every day. Their winter larder needs to be stocked with live specimens, and if we could look inside this cold and dark dungeon we would find hundreds of earthworms, the largest number found being 450 in one chamber, each unable to move but still living. The mole bites the worm's head, which incapacitates it, and a toxin in their saliva further paralyses it.

I thought of Mole, an endearing character in one of my favourite childhood books, *Wind in the Willows*. The author never mentioned this particular culinary habit which is probably just as well or a whole generation of children would have suffered nightmares for years, myself included.

So many of the most intriguing habits of the animals and birds who share this landscape with us are hidden from our eyes, sometimes literally in the ground beneath our feet. As I stock my own larder for the coming months I like to think of them busily doing exactly the same, each in their own way, although I try not to dwell too much on the underground world of the mole.

AND SO THE YEAR COMES
TO AN END

My year of asking questions has drawn to a close and, as I look back, I wonder what exactly I have learnt. This might seem an obvious question. I learnt about kingfishers and squirrels, about the sky and the wind, but the process actually taught me a great deal more than that.

When I began I didn't have any firm views on what topics would be covered, instead simply opening my mind and letting each week provide me with a question or a thought. Given my love of the outdoors, it was not surprising that so many of the themes related to the natural world but I never expected this to be so exclusively a book about nature. If I visited a city, or a museum, or a man-made wonder, thinking I might find inspiration there, I would usually walk out again, lacking that little spark that I came to recognise as the sign that my curiosity had been awakened. This project has reinforced what is most important to me, what inspires me, and that is a good thing to know.

Having been brought up on a diet of David Attenborough films I knew that the natural world could seem heartless at times. So often those documentaries relate to distant countries and to the exotic animals that inhabit them. The animals on my doorstep were far humbler but I was taken aback to find that they can be equally single-minded, sometimes even cruel, to human eyes at least, and that the line between surviving or dying is as horribly precarious in the woods around my home as it is in some far-flung jungle. The natural world has moments of great sweetness and wonder but they are tempered by times of drama and tragedy.

We humans, ever arrogant, might assume that there is little that we can learn from those creatures below us but I have found the opposite to be true. The butterfly showed me that every day is precious and should be lived with passion and intensity; the kingfisher proved that with tenacity and patience you can achieve what seems impossible. The worm taught me that beauty is only skin deep and that we all have hidden strengths and attributes that make us special, whilst the salamander and the other creatures in my pond helped me to realise the benefit of slowing down and being still sometimes. The oak taught me to be aware of how I live my life and to think about the consequences of what I leave behind. The humble sparrow proved that adaptability is the key to survival, and so many of these animals have made me painfully aware of how fragile life is, how quickly things can change, and that I should never take this precious life for granted. These are good life lessons, given by an array of wonderful teachers who live by example.

The discipline of asking these simple questions has also helped me to put some distance between myself and the wider world. These days that world is not the nicest of places and on many days I struggle to find any positive feelings about it. Much to my surprise my simple questions stood like a dam between me and all that was negative, acting as an invisible shoulder to lean on, a comforting presence that I could depend upon. I realised that if I was waiting to feel a new sense of hope about the way things were going I could be waiting a long time. Instead it is better to actively look for things that inspire and uplift us and from that it follows that we will feel better about life. Each week of being curious, of being proactive rather than reactive, of asking questions or noticing something different, was another brick in the wall, helping to hold back the endless stream of bad news and constantly reminding me that we do still live in a wonderful world if we choose our own way of looking at it.

And lastly, although this book is about nature and not about me, it has an unexpected element of the memoir about it. It has given me a snapshot collection of moments of my life, memories that I can treasure over the years. It is a great deal more than a series of facts and figures, than questions and answers. The whole has proven to be greater than the sum of its parts.

What happens now that I have reached the end of my year? I don't think I shall be able to stop asking my questions. It has become part of my routine and I don't want to go back to how it was before. I know that I could live for many more years yet and still never run out of things that can amaze me. Are you tempted to join me? Perhaps one gloomy winter's day you might find a question niggling away at the back of your mind and wonder whether to take the plunge. If you do, and I strongly recommend it, here are five simple tips that I can share now I have passed my milestone 52 questions.

The first is that it helps if you can develop the habit of noticing when a question pops into your head. We all have these questions; after all, curiosity is a part of being human, but so often we barely acknowledge them, a flicker of interest that goes as quickly as it comes. Grab that question or thought and write it down before it fades away! You don't need to do anything with it just yet, but don't lose it.

The second is to buy yourself a notebook, preferably something a bit special that you can treasure. This simple act is proof of your commitment, a sign that you are going to follow through and fill that book with what you learn, both about the world and about yourself.

The third is to carve out some time for yourself and guard it jealously. I chose to commit to an hour every Sunday morning, although it often turned out to be longer as I got drawn into my subject. If it was a cold winter's morning I would settle by the fire with a cup of tea, look at the questions or thoughts that I had jotted down during the week and pick the one that most appealed. I would browse through the internet, look at books, make a few notes and take my time. It didn't matter if I ended up with only a few lines or if it grew into pages. Neither was I concerned at this stage if it was a mishmash of words or stream of consciousness rather than a polished essay. No-one was judging me.

The fourth point is an important one. For example, you might ask a simple question about a bat or a snake but the internet will provide you with enough detail to write a book on each subject and it is all too easy to lose focus beneath the onslaught. This happened to me on numerous occasions until I learnt to concentrate on what exactly it was that I wanted to know and to discard the rest. I would rather know less, and be able to remember it, than overload myself with an excess of information. Cherry-picking the best bits in this way was my personal choice. In contrast you may find that a little information gives you an appetite to know more, to become an expert in a field that inspires you, rather than a jack of all trades like me.

And lastly, don't worry if no specific questions arise. It is enough to have a thought and give yourself time to ponder upon it, or to notice the reflections in a lake without needing to know the science behind it. This might seem a strange thing to say given the nature of this book but, whilst questions are indeed wonderful, we don't always have to search out the answers.

Please review this book

If you have enjoyed *The Language of the Badger* I would be so grateful if you could leave a review on Amazon, or Goodreads if you are a member. If you'd rather not do a written review you can easily leave a completely anonymous star rating. These personal reviews and ratings are what sell books so they really matter.

List of weekly themes

Animals
Cats
Badgers
Worms
Hares
Bats
Squirrels
Moles

Birds
Sparrows
Cranes
Grebes and geese
Terns
Storks
Magpies
Owls
Feathers
Nightingales
Kingfishers

Insects
Bees
Butterflies
Mosquitoes
Spiders
Dragonflies

Reptiles/Molluscs/Fish
Fish
Snakes
Slugs
Snails

Plants
Bluebells/cuckoo's boots
Oak tree
Tulips and bulbs
Water lily
Mushrooms and mycelium
Willow
Holly

Landscape/environmental
Silence
Pond life
Sunrise
Wilderness
Reflections
Stars
Extinction
Rainbow
Blue skies/clouds
Moon
Rivers/oceans

Weather
Wind

Seasons
Spring
Snowman
Winter

Human-related
Singing
Sense of smell
Babies
Contentment
Beauty

References

A word about references. As I cannot claim to be an expert on any of the subjects covered by this book I have carried out an extensive amount of research whilst writing it. In the reference lists below I have included my primary sources. In a bid to validate my facts I double-checked my information over many websites but where they covered the same ground as my initial sources I have not included them in these lists as they would simply become too long. I have also included a bibliography should the reader wish to improve their knowledge further.

I have done my best to ensure that my information is correct, but apologise if there are any inconsistencies or mistakes.

January

Purr-fect

www.countrylife.co.uk *Why do we say that cats have nine lives?* (6/11/22)

www.encyclopedia.com *Is it true that cats have nine lives?* (12/10/19)

www.wonderopolis.org *Wonder of the day 264*

The naming of things
www.themarginalian.org *A parliament of owls* by Marina Popova
https://www.countrylife.co.uk/ *Collective nouns for birds*
http://www.community.rspb.uk/ *Collective nouns for birds*
www.birdspot.co.uk *Collective nouns for birds*

Beauty is only skin deep
www.howstuffworks.com *How do snails get their shells*
www.molluscs.at *The Living World of Molluscs*
www.wikipedia.org *House sparrow*
www.kitchengardenfoundation.org.au *Fun facts about worms*
http://www.farmguru.org/ *15 amazing worm facts*
www.nfuonline.com *10 top facts about the earthworm*

February
Don't wish your life away
www.alimentarium.org *Candlemas – a festival of lights*
www.lincstrust.org.uk *Snowdrops*

The wild wind
Nick Hunt, 2018, *Where the Wild Winds Are: Walking Europe's Winds from the Pennines to Provence*, Nicholas Brealey Publishing, p176
www.nationalgeographic.org *Wind*
www.weatheronline.co.uk *Barber – wind of the world*
www.theconversation.com *Curious kids: Where does wind actually come from?*
www.metoffice.gov.uk *Understanding weather*
www.scienceabc.com *What generates wind*

www.farmersalmanac.com *Beware of the November Witch*
www.weatherandradar.co.uk *From West Wales to Cornwall – the return of the Pembrokeshire Dangler*
www.wikipedia.org *Black Sunday (storm)*
www.weather.gov *Dodge City – 88th anniversary of April 1935 Dust Storm (Black Sunday)*

March

The language of the badger
www.badgerland.co.uk *Detailed badger sounds*
www.wildlifeonline.me.uk *European Badger Behaviour*
www.badgertrust.org.uk

Spring is in the air
www.imagine@theconversation *Climate change is warping the seasons*
www.birdsandblooms.com *Why do birds sing in spring?*
www.daysontheclaise.blogspot *The sound of cranes flying*

Buzz
www.brittanica.com *Why do bees buzz?*
www.buzzaboutbees.net *Why do bees buzz*
www.worldhoneymarket.com *The science behind bees' buzz*

Cuckoo's boots
www.woodlandtrust.org.uk *Bluebells*

Heady scents
www.smithsonianmag.com *Sniffing out the science of smelling*

www.fifthsense.org.uk *How smell works*

www.nidcd.nih.gov/health *Smell disorders*

April

The dance of the butterflies

www.nhm.ac.uk *Love is in the air: how butterflies date*

www.discoverwildlife.com *The butterfly lifecycle explained*

Legacy

https://www.woodlandtrust.org.uk/ *Oak trees and wildlife*

May

Fishy feelings

www.freedomforanimals.org.uk *Fish have feelings too*

www.spca.bc.ca *Fun facts about fish*

www.thehumaneleague.org.uk *11 amazing facts you probably didn't know about fish*

What lies beneath?

www.dutchgrown.com *The life cycle of your flower bulbs*

Fending for ourselves

www.livescience.com *Why are babies helpless?*

www.sciencenorway.no *This is why humans are born completely helpless*

www.wildnatureblog.wordpress.com *On late nesting great crested grebes*

www.wikipedia.org *Greylag goose*

A nightingale sang

www.discoverwildlife.com *10 amazing facts about nightingales*

www.a-z-animals.com *Nightingale*

June

How do you measure something you can't see?

www.en.m.wikipedia.org *Beaufort Scales*

Stormy days

www.wwt.org.uk *Can birds survive devastating storms?*

www.allaboutbirds.org *How do birds survive in very cold temperatures* and also *How do small birds do in a storm?*

http://www.audubon.org/ *Gimme shelter – how do birds survive a snow storm?*

Thief

www.nhm.ac.uk (Natural History Museum) *Curious collectors and hoarders of the animal world*

www.discoverwildlife.com *How to identify bird egg thieves*

www.treehugger.com *Kleptoparasites: 8 animals that steal from others*

July

The elusive kingfisher

www.scottishwildlifetrust.org.uk *How does a kingfisher build its nest?*

www.allaboutbirds.org *Belted kingfisher – Life history*

www.discoverwildlife.com *Kingfisher guide – special facts and best place to see* www.wikipedia.org *Common kingfisher*

Watching me, watching you
www.woodlandtrust.org.uk *Why do hares box?*
wildlifephotographic.blogspot.com *Just hare necessities*
www.animalwised.com *Rabbit vision v human vision*

Water lily
www.almanac.com *Birth month flowers*
www.bloomandwild.com *Birth month flowers*

Cruel to be kind
www.worldwidebirder.com *Why do storks kill their young?*
www.rewildingbritain.org.uk *White stork*
https://scienceinpoland.pl/en *Stork nests*
www.livescience.com *What's behind the myth that storks deliver babies?*
www.delokkerij.nl *Visit to a stork breeding station*

August

Wondrous willow
www.treesforlife.org.uk *Willow tree mythology and folklore*
www.aspirin-foundation.com *The Aspirin Story*

Dancing jewel
www.british-dragonflies.org.uk *Frequently asked questions (odonta)*
www.treehugger.com *Things you never knew about dragonflies*
www.community.rspb.uk

www.pondlife.me.uk *Dragonflies*

One for sorrow
www.livingwithbirds.com *21 wildlife facts on magpies*
www.rte.ie *One for sorrow one for joy*
www.blog.lovegardenbirds.co.uk *Wise Owl Blog: Magpie superstitions*
www.arkwildlife.co.uk *British Magpie: habitat food and identification*

Suppose we weren't here
www.theconversation.com *If humans went extinct, what would the world look like after one year?*

September

Celestial beast
https://www.skyatnightmagazine.com *A complete guide to observing The Plough in the night sky*
www.woodland-ways.co.uk *Bushcraft – The Great Bear*

Snake in the grass
www.welcomewildlife.com *Interesting facts about snakes*
www.everythingreptiles.com *23 fun and interesting snake facts and statistics*
www.woodlandtrust.org.uk *Grass snakes*
www.en.m.wikipedia.org *Snakes in mythology*
Recommended reading: *The Book of Snakes: A life-size guide to six hundred species from around the world* by Mark O'Shea

Blind as a bat

www.discoverwildlife.com *Various article on bats*

www.bats.org.uk (Bat Conservation Trust) *About bats*

www.wildlifeonline.me.uk *What is echolocation?*

The wood wide web

www.fungially.com *What is mycelium – nature's worldwide web underneath our feet*

www.urbantreefestival.org *How trees communicate*

www.fantasticfungi.com *10 things to know about the mycelial network*

www.kew.org (Royal Botanic Gardens) *Mycelium: exploring the hidden dimensions of fungus*

October

Are owls really wise?

www.newscientist.com *Are owls really intelligent?*

www.owlpages.com *Owls in mythology and culture*

Slug love

www.wikipedia.org *Mating of gastropods*

www.naturetalksandwalks.co.uk

www.jic.ac.uk/research (John Innes Centre) *All about slugs*

www.nematodesdirect.co.uk

Water, water everywhere

www.wikipedia.org *Message in a bottle*

Pointless existence

www.nationalgeographic.com *Mosquitoes*

November

Can we make things better?

www.earth.com *UN Report – Alarming details about current status of Earth's wildlife*

www.discovermagazine.com *What animals are going extinct*

www.nhm.ac.uk (Natural History Museum) *What is mass extinction and are we facing a sixth one?*

http://wwf.panda.org/ *How many species are we losing?*

www.rspb.org.uk *How it started – the female campaigners who created the RSPB*

www.fashioningfeathers.info *Murderous Millinery*

Flight of the spiderlings

www.treehugger.com *Captivating facts about spider silk*

www.discoverwildlife.com *Facts about spiders*

https://www.woodlandtrust.org.uk/ *Why do spiders make webs*

www.a-z-animals.com/blog *The largest spider web ever found*

www.westernexterminator.com *Ten facts about spiders*

A day of gifts

www.treehugger.com *20 amazing facts about feathers 5/5/2020*

www.theguardian.com *Neurophilosophy: Birds pack more cells into their brains than mammals 15/6/2016*

Pot of gold

www.irelandbeforeyoudie.com *10 best things you never knew about leprechauns (2024)*

December

Head in the clouds

www.space.com

www.howstuffworks.com *Why is the sky blue?*

www.metoffice.gov.uk

https://cloudappreciationsociety.org

www.ted.com/talks *Gavin Pretor-Pinney*

The moon of the long night

www.rmg.co.uk/stories (Royal Museums Greenwich) *What is a blue moon?*

www.timeanddate/astronomy.com

Holly

www.treesforlife.org.uk *Holly – mythology and folklore*

www.woodlandtrust.org.uk *Holly*

Winter larder

www.treehugger.com *Surprising ways animals stock up for winter*

BIBLIOGRAPHY

An Unkindness of Ravens: A Book of Collective Nouns by Chloe Rhodes

Every Day Nature: How noticing nature can quietly change your life by Andy Beer

Where the Wild Winds Are: Walking Europe's Winds from the Pennines to Provence by Nick Hunt

50 years of Wildlife Photographer of the Year: How Wildlife Photography Became Art by the Natural History Museum

Badger Behaviour, Conservation and Rehabilitation: 70 years of Getting to Know Badgers by George E Pearce

What a Fish Knows: The Inner Lives of Our Underwater Cousins by Jonathan Balcombe

The Way of the Hare by Marianne Taylor

The Hidden Life of Trees: What They Feel, How They Communicate by Peter Wohlleben

Finding the Mother Tree: Uncovering the Wisdom and Intelligence of the Forest by Suzanne Simard

What an Owl Knows by Jennifer Ackerman

The History of the Snowman by Bob Eckstein

Acknowledgements

My grateful thanks to the team as always: Louise Lubke Cuss at Wordblink for her copyediting, Georgia Laval at Laval Editing for formatting and Ebook Launch for the cover design. A special mention for Helen Isaacs who is my beta reader and provides invaluable advice and support along the way and thank you to friends and family who helped choose the title. And of course a big thank you to my husband Michael for providing the stunning drawings – they bring the animals and birds that are the star of the show to life.

About the author

In 2017 Mary-Jane and her husband Michael sold their house in Wales and bought a boat called *Olivia Rose*, determined to leave the rat race behind and find a better life. Three years later they also bought a one-room, off-grid cabin in the south west of France and made France their home. Now they split their time between cruising through Europe in summer and exploring around their home in winter.

Mary-Jane has written a series of four books about their lives and travels. *Just Passing Through* and *The Constant Traveller* are a record of their years on the water, following their ups and downs as they find out whether a life afloat is as idyllic as they had hoped it would be. *The Turning of the Seasons* is the prequel, set in Wales when they lived a smallholding life and explains how they came to leave it all behind. *A Simple Life* shares the adventure of living off-grid, learning a new perspective and reconnecting to the natural world.

The Language of the Badger marks a new direction, moving away from travel writing into nature writing.

A love of nature and the outdoors is a common theme through all her books, as is the idea that a simple life can be incredibly satisfying and enriching. Mary-Jane writes a regular blog at www.theoliviarosediaries.com.

EXCERPT FROM *A SIMPLE LIFE*

Foreword

Opportunities

I think many of the big changes that people make to their lives happen by chance. An opportunity will drift past us, often when we least expect it, and we must decide whether to take it, or let it go. If we take it, our lives may change dramatically. If we let it go, our lives drift on and we will never know if we have missed out on something magical or avoided a catastrophe.

Our decision to try our hand at living an off-grid life in France was one of those opportunities. It came at the right time, in the right place, although we weren't looking for it and, in many ways, didn't want it. My husband Michael and I thought we had our life all sorted out. We had made our really big life-changing decision three years previously, selling our house and closing our business down. Now we lived a nomadic life, either on our boat in France, in our caravan in the UK, or travelling in our campervan. We split our time between Europe and the UK and it was all we ever wanted.

But life is like a river, sometimes calm, sometimes unpredictable and turbulent, and you never know what is around the next corner. In 2020 we foundered upon the Brexit rock. No longer able to live and move freely between Europe and the UK, we had to make a choice. We chose France.

Although we had no desire to buy another home, without it we would not be able to stay in France for more than three months out of every six. If we had bought a conventional house I think it would have meant little to us, being no more than a means to an end, allowing us to continue living in the way we had chosen, but by chance we found an off-grid, one-room wooden cabin in the Pyrénées-Atlantiques region of France. It had no electricity, no kitchen, no bathroom or bedroom, and the loo was a bucket in a shed, but it came with five acres of field and woodland. The idea of living off-grid on our own land appealed to us and so the deal was done.

I have followed my dreams in the past and some of them have turned out to be less than I had hoped for. This tiny cabin wasn't a dream at all, just a solution to a problem, a part-time home for the winter which would allow us to spend the summers on our boat, and yet it enriched my life in ways I could never have foreseen. Off-grid living in itself proved to be a revelation, and we fitted together like hand and glove, but it was so much more than that. We were living in *la France profonde*, deep in the heart of rural France, where wild boar and deer still roamed the forests, where pockets of the natural world were still untamed and where mankind could at times feel utterly, wonderfully insignificant. No-one had lived in our cabin for at least a year and the wildlife had taken over by the time we arrived. Every day brought something new to marvel at: deer browsing in our field at dusk and dawn, salamanders on the doorstep, a praying mantis in the vegetable bed, vast, swirling migrations of wood pigeons filling the sky, birdsong by day and owls calling by night. I felt like a child again, the world full of possibilities and endless questions that needed answers.

If our own little world felt magical, the world outside was far from it. As well as working out how to construct our off-grid power system of solar panels and batteries, we had to negotiate our way through the Brexit paper trail, rearranging key elements of our lives. We also had to learn the French way of doing things, to begin the long process of integrating more deeply into French society than we had previously. In many ways this was a positive experience, but at times the French love-hate relationship with paperwork and bureaucracy was challenging. Worst of all was the fact that we were living through the Covid-19 pandemic, with all the worry and uncertainty that came with it.

When I began writing this book I thought the main theme would be off-grid living, but other elements have elbowed their way into the limelight and now share the pages. How could I ignore the wildlife who share our little patch of land? Or not be aware that we have a responsibility to manage our field and woods for this wildlife as well as for ourselves? I hope this book portrays a growing and enduring love for the richness of the natural world and a gratitude for the succour it gives when the outside world becomes a frightening place. And, last but not least, France and her people are also included as we learn about the country's traditions old and new, and come to better understand the French way of viewing the world.

I can't think of a time in my life when there has been such uncertainty on so many levels, when people across the world are reassessing both how they live their lives and what really matters to them. Change is in the air, and it seems this move to a simpler, more pared-down way of life couldn't have come at a more relevant time.

Chapter 1

Coming to terms with a new situation

'This is ridiculous,' I muttered crossly to myself as we followed the estate agent's car through the winding lanes. 'Why should we have to buy a house just so that we can stay on our boat?'

'We're buying a house so that we can stay in the country,' said Michael. 'How long we spend in it is down to us.'

'Well, it's stupid. I don't want a house.'

'Neither do I. But we at least have to look at this one. It'll probably be no good anyway.'

A few minutes later we arrived at the property. A gravel driveway led off the single-track lane and then petered out, swamped by grass and bracken almost waist-high in places. Someone had recently cut a swathe through this wilderness and the resulting track led across the field and then disappeared down a slight incline. I could just see the hint of a tiled roof at the far end.

We followed the estate agent across the field. He was immaculate in a white shirt, beautifully cut trousers and designer sunglasses and looked out of place, an urban creature dropped into a jungle. The wooden cabin was hunkered down at the end of the track, a single storey building with a sloping roof. A massive ash tree towered over it, blocking out most of the sunlight and as we went in I shivered, even though it was a hot July day. It was dark inside and smelt of petrol fumes. As my eyes grew accustomed to the gloom I saw a strimmer on the floor. That would explain the smell. It was sparsely furnished, a dining table and four chairs, a small armchair, a couple of wardrobes. Three cardboard boxes sat on top of the slatted base of a single bed. The middle-aged lady who had lived here alone had died in hospital from cancer over a year ago. Her remaining family, two sisters, lived far away and it was her nephew who kept an eye on the place and had tidied things up for the viewing.

Being an off-grid property there was no electricity so we couldn't turn the lights on. There was a line of narrow windows above the front door, up close to where the wall met the top of the sloping ceiling, a strange design feature in that they couldn't be opened without a ladder, but the sun had moved around and little light was coming through them at this time of the day. The French patio doors were north facing and refused to budge when the estate agent tentatively tried to open them.

A woodburner squatted in the middle of the far wall, which consisted of a minimal number of stone pebbles set in an overwhelming amount of cement, a typical feature of the rural buildings in this part of the country. It was the one remaining wall of what had been a forge many years ago and was the reason why planning permission had been granted to build the cabin around it. A crack zig-zagged through it from top to bottom immediately behind the woodburner. The three remaining walls and the ceiling were made from wood.

A large galvanised bucket filled one corner of the room, bolted to the floor, with a plughole and drainage to the outside. There were no taps or any other plumbing.

'Is this for washing clothes?' I asked the agent.

'*Non*, for a shower,' came the response.

I looked at him, eyebrows raised.

He shrugged. 'The lady who lived here, she was quite a character from what I hear. I should like to have met her.'

Coming back outside again, blinking owlishly in the bright sunshine, we found a small greenhouse, squeezed into the space just to the right of the front door, and a ramshackle collection of sheds on the other side of it. The largest had a selection of rusty tools propped up in one corner and three cords of thick string stretched across from one side of the ceiling to the other. It had previously been used as an indoor washing line, but a creeper had found its way in through a gap in the wooden-slatted walls and taken it over, twining and tangling its way along the entire length, with just a few splashes of colour from half-hidden plastic pegs to give the clue to what had been there before. The smallest of the sheds was the outside composting toilet, a narrow space just wide enough to take the wooden frame holding the loo seat with the bucket beneath it. Spiders' webs were everywhere, cunningly placed in corners, artistically strung between the wooden beams of the ceiling, even across the doors, leaving me in no doubt as to who was now in charge of this space. On the other side of the cabin, by the patio doors, was an open-fronted shed with an outside sink and draining board. Welcome to the kitchen.

The estate agent was a straight-talker. He said that he didn't think much of the cabin, but the real value lay in the land. A good-sized field with adjoining woodland in such a lovely location was hard to come by, especially at the price on offer. At 33,000€ the family had priced it for a quick sale.

We told him we would have a think about it and went our separate ways.

Driving back I could sense Michael looking at me.

'You're not saying much.'

'No.'

'What do you think?'

'I don't know.'

But I did know. Or at least my head knew; my heart just hadn't caught up with the reality of it yet. If we wanted to stay in France for more than three months in every six, which would be the new regime from January 1st 2021 when full-Brexit kicked in, we needed to be able to prove that we were resident and buying a property was the best way to do it. We also needed to do this quickly because the financial requirements that would allow us to stay were currently low and within our earning capability. After the end of this year, everything would change and not in our favour. I told myself that just because we had a house didn't mean we had to spend all our time in it. We could still have the long summers cruising on the boat, and split the winter visiting family, staying in our new home for just a few months and escaping in the campervan to nearby Spain for a couple of weeks if we needed a dose of winter sunshine. It wasn't what we wanted or would have chosen but, given the situation, it all made sense. If we wanted to stay in France, this was the only way.

My problem was that it didn't feel right. I loved the way we lived our life. I loved the freedom that comes when you are not tied to any one place, when all the places that you call home, in our case a boat, a caravan and a campervan, are mobile. Your house is on your back and it goes where you go. It feels as if the entire world is an open, welcoming space without boundaries and life is full of possibilities. I loved the freedom that comes from having few possessions, few responsibilities. I loved everything about my life and I didn't want anything else. Buying a house, even one like this, a one-room-does-all slightly decrepit shack, felt like a step backwards towards a life I thought I had left behind. It wasn't the off-grid nature of it that was a problem, in fact that was one of the more appealing aspects. I simply didn't want to be tied down.

We went back to look at it again the next day, just by ourselves so we could take our time and try to get a feel for the place. Michael fought his way up the slope of the field in search of the two plots of woodland that went with the cabin, our dog Maddie at his heels, the top of her head all I could see through the long grass, whilst I wandered round the garden, not that you could call it that for most of it was buried under brambles. There were a couple of raised beds where the previous owner had grown her vegetables, now mostly stifled by weeds, but a lone bay tree remained. A couple of clay flowerpots, mottled with age, suggested that there had been geraniums in summers past, and an old wicker basket chair sat crookedly off-balance in the grass by the track. An image of the previous owner flashed into my mind, sitting there in the chair in the sunshine, resting after weeding her vegetables.

Despite the overwhelming air of abandonment, with everything falling into disrepair, I had a sudden sense that this place had once been loved and cared for. I looked over the hedge, my eyes following the contours down into the valley floor below, golden with maize and sunflowers, and then lifting slowly to the horizon, past the small hamlets on the other side of the valley, terracotta roofs and red shutters warm in the sunshine, and then on up to the wooded slopes behind them. If I turned to the south, I could see the Pyrenees just forty kilometres away, majestic even from this distance, sharply etched against a cornflower-blue sky.

I shut my eyes and listened. Birdsong and bees. No traffic, no people. The sound of a dog barking in the distance. I could hear Michael and Maddie working their way back down the field and opened my eyes again.

'Did you find anything?' I asked.

'Nope. I can't get through. The brambles are above my head.'

We put an offer in the next day. It was accepted. There was no going back now.

Within a week I found that my heart had caught up with my head. I could see that this was an opportunity and that I needed to get over my fear that it would tie us down. There was no reason for it to impinge on our free-moving lifestyle; rather it was just another place out of many for us to spend time and, instead of feeling irritated that Brexit had forced this upon us, I should embrace this new facet of our lives. We began to get excited about putting in the off-grid system, reclaiming the garden, and exploring the valleys and woods nearby and the Pyrenees so close to our doorstep.

It was our intention to be landlubbers for no more than four or five months of the year, during the winter. Our summers would still be aboard *Olivia Rose*, and we would bring the caravan over to France and live in it while we made the necessary changes to the cabin. This wasn't going to be an onerous start-from-scratch project. We wanted to keep it simple, in keeping with the principles of off-grid living. And it was only one room after all. How hard could it be?

We moved in on September 21st, just two and a half months after the day we first saw it, one of the quickest and easiest property purchases we had ever gone through, a good omen for the future. A new chapter in our lives had begun.

Printed in Great Britain
by Amazon

60174835R00129